AF248600

The Modern Poet

The Modern Poet

an Anthology chosen and edited

by

GWENDOLEN MURPHY

London: Sidgwick & Jackson, Ltd.
44 Museum Street, W.C.1

First published, May, 1938
Reprinted, July, 1938
July, 1942
October, 1943
April, 1944
April, 1945
December, 1945
December, 1946
April, 1947
August, 1948
August, 1954

PRINTED AND BOUND IN ENGLAND BY
HAZELL WATSON AND VINEY LTD
AYLESBURY AND LONDON

PREFACE

This book has been planned with a view to illustrating the change that has come over English poetry in the last two decades. It exemplifies poetic ideals and characteristics strikingly dissimilar to those of the " Georgians." This attempt to delimit the province of modern poetry will be seen to be a question not of date but of spirit. The editor's selective principle has been to show the quality and excellence of modern poetry.

Based as it is mainly on the work of living poets, from America as well as from the British Isles, it includes valuable explanations and comments secured by the editor from some of the poets themselves. Thereby it constitutes a document of unique critical value, as well as being an anthology, which should appeal both to the reader already familiar with modern poetry and to those who desire to know more of it.

Teachers will find, however, that at the same time the needs of schools and of classes in adult education have been kept in mind throughout. In various instances the editor's final choice between poems of equal merit has been determined after consultation with lecturers in English, with practical teachers, and teachers of verse-speaking.

ACKNOWLEDGEMENTS

MANY besides myself will be grateful to those poets who, when consulted about the meaning of poems or parts of poems, co-operated generously. I would especially thank Miss Laura Riding and Mr. Robert Graves for the help they have given, not only in explaining their poems, but in discussing the value of poetry and its communication ; Miss Riding has written a valuable account of the poet at work, printed under her name in the notes. My thanks are also due to Mr. Michael Roberts for his general sympathy as well as for his help in the comments on his poetry and his interesting account of the symbolism of *The Castle* ; to Mr. Edwin Muir for his stimulating story of the origins of *The Riders* ; to Mr. Ronald Bottrall for his readiness in explaining parts of his poems ; to Mr. Richard Church for his illuminating comment on *Secret Service* ; to Mr. E. C. Bentley for the first and attractive definition of " clerihew " ; to Mr. Charles Madge and Mr. David Gascoyne for help in throwing light on the background of their poetry ; and to Mr. W. B. Yeats for interesting notes on his *Byzantium*.

In certain instances the poets have suggested slight divergences from the texts of their poems as previously published, and these I have been glad to incorporate. At least ten poems are here published for the first time.

Much gratitude is also due to friends : to Miss E. Seaton and Miss M. St. C. Byrne for their ready and generous advice, and in addition in particular to Miss Seaton for discussing the proofs with me, and to Miss Byrne for introducing me to Don Marquis ; to Miss H. F. Brettell, Miss A. Miller and Miss E. Tisdall for discussing the choice of poems.   G. M.

For permission to use copyright poems the editor and publishers are greatly indebted to the authors ; to the literary executors of J. Freeman (Mrs. Freeman), G. M. Hopkins (the poet's family), D. H. Lawrence (Mrs. Lawrence), V. Lindsay (Mrs. Lindsay), D. Marquis (Miss B. Marquis), Charlotte Mew and Harold Monro (Mrs. Monro and the Poetry Bookshop), W. Owen (Mrs. Susan Owen), I. Rosenberg (Mrs. Wynick), E. Thomas (Mrs. Thomas) ; and to the following publishers in respect of the poems enumerated :

The Cambridge University Press :
Frances Cornford, *Mountains and Molehills* (Nos. 35, 36).

Messrs. Jonathan Cape Ltd. :
A. E. Housman, *More Poems* (No. 6).
Laura Riding, *Poems : A Joking Word* (No. 67).
M. Roberts, *Poems* (Nos. 73, 74).

Messrs. Chatto & Windus :
H. D., *Red Roses for Bronze* (Nos. 37, 38).
W. Empson, *Poems* (No. 86).
W. Owen, *Poems* (Nos. 54, 55).
I. Rosenberg, *Poems* (No. 49).

Messrs. R. Cobden-Sanderson Ltd. :
E. Blunden, *Choice and Chance* (No. 60).
H. Monro, *Collected Poems* (Nos. 21, 22, 23, 24).
A Porter, *The Signature of Pain* (No. 59).

Messrs. Constable & Co. Ltd. :
W. de la Mare, *Peacock Pie* (No. 13).
          Motley and Other Poems (No. 14).

Messrs. J. M. Dent & Sons, Ltd. :
C. Dyment, *Straight or Curly ?* (No. 101).
E. Muir, *Variations on a Time Theme* (No. 40).
D. Thomas, *Twenty-Five Poems* (No. 100).

Messrs. Gerald Duckworth & Co., Ltd. :
    Edith Sitwell, *Collected Poems* (No. 41).
    O. Sitwell, *Collected Satires and Poems* (No. 51).

Messrs. Faber & Faber Ltd. :
    W. H. Auden, *Look Stranger !* (No. 84).
                    Letters from Iceland (No. 85).
    T. S. Eliot, *Collected Poems, 1909-1935* (Nos. 44, 45, 46).
    L. MacNeice, *Poems* (Nos. 88, 89).
    C. Madge, *The Disappearing Castle* (No. 99).
    D. Marquis, *archy and mehitabel* (No. 19).
    Marianne Moore, *Selected Poems* (Nos. 42, 43).
    E. Pound, *Selected Poems* (Nos. 27, 28).
                    A Draft of XXX Cantos (No. 29).
    H. Read, *Poems, 1914-1934* (p. xx of Introduction).
    S. Spender, *Poems* (No. 94).
    E. Thomas, *Collected Poems* (Nos. 15, 16, 17, 18).

Mr. Gordon Fraser :
    R. Bottrall, *The Loosening* (Nos. 80, 81 and p. xix of Intro-
    duction).

Messrs. Wm. Heinemann, Ltd. :
    R. Graves, *Poems, 1926-1930* (No. 61).
    D. H. Lawrence, *Collected Poems* (Nos. 31, 33, 34).
                    Last Poems (No. 30).
                    Pansies (No. 32).

The Hogarth Press :
    J. Lehmann, *New Signatures* (No. 90).
                    The Noise of History (No. 91).
    C. Day Lewis, *A Time to Dance* (No. 78).
                    The Magnetic Mountain (No. 77).
    J. C. Ransom, *Grace after Meat* (Nos. 47, 48).
    Victoria Sackville-West, *Collected Poems* (Nos. 52, 53).
    S. Spender, *New Signatures* (No. 93).
    A. S. J. Tessimond, *New Signatures* (No. 76).

Messrs. Alfred A. Knopf :
    Elinor Wylie, *Collected Poems* (No. 39).

The Macmillan Company :
  V. Lindsay, *Collected Poems* (No. 20).

Messrs. Macmillan & Co. Ltd. :
  J. Freeman, *Last Poems* (No. 25).
  W. B. Yeats, *Collected Poems* (Nos. 7, 8, 9, 10).

The Parton Press :
  E. E. Cummings, *1/20 Poems* (No. 58).

The Oxford University Press :
  G. M. Hopkins, *Poems* (Nos. 1, 2, 3, 4, 5).

The Seizin Press and Messrs. Constable & Co., Ltd. :
  N. Cameron, *Epilogue*, Vol. III, Spring 1937 (No. 79).
  R. Graves, *Epilogue*, Vol. II, Summer 1936 (No. 65).
      Epilogue, Vol. III, Spring 1937 (No. 66).
      To Whom Else ? (Nos. 62, 63).
  A. Hodge, *Epilogue*, Vol. III, Spring 1937 (No. 102).
  J. Reeves, *The Natural Need* (No. 95).

Messrs. Sidgwick & Jackson, Ltd. :
  H. Asquith, *Poems, 1912-1933* (No. 26).

Grateful acknowledgement is also made to the Editor of *Life and
Letters* for permission to reprint *Mud* (No. 56), by R. Church ; to
the Editor of *The Listener* for permission to reprint *The Witnesses*
(No. 83), by W. H. Auden, *The Unattained* (No. 103), by D. Gascoyne,
Blocking the Pass (No. 98), by C. Madge, *Song* (No. 87), by L. Mac-
Neice, *The Castle* (No. 75), by M. Roberts ; to the Editor of *New
Verse* for permission to reprint *This poem will be you . . .* (p. xvii of
Introduction), by C. Madge, and *Fata Morgana* (No. 92), by K. J.
Raine ; to the Editors of *Scrutiny* for permission to reprint *Preamble
to a Great Adventure* (No. 82), by R. Bottrall.

THE MODERN POET

INTRODUCTION

THE far-reaching disturbances resulting from the Great War have accelerated changes in thought and in habits in all directions. In the poetic tradition the way has been made clearer for a wider and more energetic view of life in all its aspects. This has become so much the outstanding characteristic of modern poetry that it has been said, and with much truth, that no anthology can rightly be described as modern which includes the comparatively timid Georgians.

It is fascinating, in reading a group of modern poems, to become aware of the spirit that they have in common : to see how poets of opposite views are yet one in their insistence upon being of their time, and how poets born generations ago may yet be of the company.

The reputed difficulty of modern poetry has prevented some of it from being read. But difficulty may mean great seriousness or great beauty, so that we lose much by being repelled by it. A poem at first apparently obscure may prove rich in things that can become our possessions for life. *The Windhover* (no. 1) is an example : the power of the poem can be felt before it is "understood." It can be discussed because of its richness, time after time, with ever-increasing interest.

Gerard Manley Hopkins again and again stresses his counsel that his poems, especially the most complicated, should be read aloud. He wrote to Bridges on February 10, 1888:

" Dearest Bridges,

. . . I laughed outright and often, but very sardonically, to think you and the Canon [1] could not construe my last sonnet ; that he had to write to you for a crib. . . . if you and he cannot understand me who will? Yet, declaimed, the strange constructions would be dramatic and effective."

G. M. H.

Similarly, a recent critic [2] has expressed himself as " all thankful " that he was first introduced to T. S. Eliot's poetry by hearing it read aloud, so that he was thus enabled " to feel from the outset its lyric sound and movement, instead of losing the poetry in a tortuous effort to find a logical pattern in its unfamiliar structure."

Another point of view is Laura Riding's, who is convinced that there is considerable disagreement among poets as to how much of the meaning of a poem can be caught by reading it aloud, and the part that sound plays in its structure. W. B. Yeats lays a major stress on the sound-element ; Laura

[1] R. W. Dixon.
[2] F. O. Matthiesen, in *The Achievement of T. S. Eliot* (preface), 1935.

Riding insists, oppositely, "that in a poem sound properly disappears, that the voice-element of the sound should be absorbed, in the varied inflections of thought that the poem induces in our mind when we read it, and that the enunciation element—the sensitive way in which words as combinations of letters are inter-related—should serve the function in reading, of sharpening our emotional attention to the poem's requirements."

But she would agree with Hopkins that "a difficult poem when read aloud can—if it is a good one—show itself to be a unified piece of work, not just a medley of obscure phrases."

At any rate, whether we read a poem aloud or not, we must be prepared to take it as it comes : not to resist its general effect by boggling at details. A poem by Charles Madge [1] speaks of the emotional stimulation to be got by running " high-speed " with a poem :

This poem will be you if you will.   So let it.
    I do not want you to stand still to get it.
You will have it if you go high-speed ; it slides in
Between velocities ; you will not need to begin
But to have begun and to be going ; to have started
To be not separate but flowing ; not to be parted
From the smooth spate ; be in action ; and be there
Not because you are a fraction, but anywhere
Let all and you be all and in relation. . . .

[1] See notes, p. 200.

Not as a thrown-in stone fall ; separation
Is standstill ; that is breakdown ; that is the end ;
You cannot get it so ; cannot make and cannot spend
When we fall sick, heart stops, and no more breath
But when the moment a stone drops, that is death.

The subjects of modern poetry are new chiefly in the sense that the old frames are newly filled. The dark night of the soul, the Hound of Heaven, philosophy, social problems, time itself, disintegration of the old, an uncertain future—are treated as if for the first time. But still newer is Science, whether as psychology and dreams, or chemistry and geology. What is figured by "iron implements," "magnetic apparatus," and "the telephone" ?—the surprising answer is "an Almond Tree ! "[1] And there is also machinery, with "cranes," "the shriek of brakes," "peering drills," "tungstyle needles," and "hypodermic syringes." Such word-tests would readily differentiate a modern collection from one of even a few years ago.

Dramatic eclogue and monologue are with us again ; satire finds new subjects, and wit is coming back ; but there is much less nature poetry, and when it is there it is used as a symbol. For modern poetry is constantly significant.

Ronald Bottrall, however, reminds us that though the subjects of modern poetry are new, links with tradition are still there :

See no. 34, *Bare Almond Trees* (D. H. Lawrence).

THE THYRSUS RETIPPED [1]

NIGHTINGALES, Anangke, a sunset or the meanest
        flower
Were formerly the potentialities of poetry,
But now what have they to do with one another
With Dionysus or with me ?

Drawn for a time towards inept vivisection
I learned to air profundity in a comment
As well by understudying Joyce as Valéry,
Both sorting ill with my bent.

Too bewildered to seek anew my element
I have lain supine, as Shelley lay questing truth on
The cool bottom of an untrampled pool,
Oddly enamoured of his marine prison.

Microscopic anatomy of ephemerides,
Power-house stacks, girder-ribs, provide a crude base
But man is what he eats, and they are not bred
Flesh of our flesh, being unrelated
Experientially, fused in no emotive furnace.

Hints for a prosthesis
Are, finding once more half-shivered laughs
In the suspense of a key turned in a corridor lock,
Or the strangeness of a snatched kiss—
These not to be read as epitaphs.

[1] See notes, pp. 192–4.

In the following poem Herbert Read [1] refers to the gradual giving-up of the old conventional themes, recognising nevertheless their recurrence and their beauty.

DAY'S AFFIRMATION

EMERGING at midnight
    to cool my aching eyes with the sight of stars
I hear the nightingale
throbbing in the thicket by my garden gate

and I think
A poet in the old days would have made a song
of your song and the starlit night
the scent of wallflowers clinging to the ground.

But now it is different :
you sing but we are silent
our hearts too sadly patient
all these years.

Sing on !   The night is cool.
Morning and the world will be lit
with whitebeam candles shining and O the frail
and tender daring splendour of wild cherrytrees.

See notes, p. 179.

THE MODERN POET

1. THE WINDHOVER

To Christ our Lord

I CAUGHT this morning morning's minion, king-
    dom of daylight's dauphin, dapple-dawn-drawn
        Falcon, in his riding
Of the rolling level underneath him steady air, and
    striding
High there, how he rung upon the rein of a wimpling
                                                wing
In his ecstasy ! then off, off forth on swing,
    As a skate's heel sweeps smooth on a bow-bend : the
        hurl and gliding
    Rebuffed the big wind. My heart in hiding
Stirred for a bird,—the achieve of, the mastery of the
    thing !

Brute beauty and valour and act, oh, air, pride, plume,
                                                here
Buckle ! AND the fire that breaks from thee then, a
    billion
Times told lovelier, more dangerous, O my chevalier !

M.P.—I

No wonder of it : shéer plód makes plough down sillion
Shine, and blue-bleak embers, ah my dear,
    Fall, gall themselves, and gash gold-vermilion.
Gerard Manley Hopkins.

2. HEAVEN—HAVEN

A nun takes the veil

I HAVE desired to go
    Where springs not fail,
To fields where flies no sharp and sided hail
    And a few lilies blow.

And I have asked to be
    Where no storms come,
Where the green swell is in the havens dumb,
    And out of the swing of the sea.
Gerard Manley Hopkins.

3. HURRAHING IN HARVEST

SUMMER ends now ; now, barbarous in beauty, the
    stooks arise
Around ; up above, what wind-walks ! What lovely
    behaviour
Of silk-sack clouds ! has wilder, wilful-wavier
Meal-drift moulded ever and melted across skies ?

I walk, I lift up, I lift up heart, eyes,
Down all that glory in the heavens to glean our
    Saviour ;
And, éyes, heárt, what looks, what lips yet gave you a
Rapturous love's greeting of realer, of rounder replies ?

And the azurous hung hills are his world-wielding
    shoulder
Majestic—as a stallion stalwart, very-violet-sweet!—
These things, these things were here and but the
    beholder
Wanting ; which two when they once meet,
The heart rears wings bold and bolder
    And hurls for him, O half hurls earth for him off
    under his feet.

                    Gerard Manley Hopkins.

4. CARRION COMFORT

Not, I'll not, carrion comfort, Despair, not feast on
    thee ;
Not untwist—slack they may be—these last strands of
    man
In me ór, most weary, cry *I can no more.* I can ;
Can something, hope, wish day come, not choose not to
    be.
But ah, but O thou terrible, why wouldst thou rude on
    me
Thy wring-world right foot rock? lay a lion limb against
    me ? scan
With darksome devouring eyes my bruisèd bones ?
    and fan,
O in turns of tempest, me heaped there ; me frantic to
    avoid thee and flee ?
Why ? That my chaff might fly ; my grain lie, sheer
    and clear.
Nay in all that toil, that coil, since (seems) I kissed the
    rod,

Hand rather, my heart lo ! lapped strength, stole joy,
    would laugh, chéer.
Cheer whom though ? the hero whose heaven-handling
    flung me, fóot tród
Me ? or me that fought him ? O which one ? is it each
    one ?   That night, that year
Of now done darkness I wretch lay wrestling with (my
    God !) my God.

Gerard Manley Hopkins.

5. NO WORST, THERE IS NONE ..

No worst, there is none. Pitched past pitch of
    grief,
More pangs will, schooled at forepangs, wilder wring.
Comforter, where, where is your comforting ?
Mary, mother of us, where is your relief ?
My cries heave, herds-long ; huddle in a main, a chief
Woe, world-sorrow ; on an age-old anvil wince and
sing—
Then lull, then leave off. Fury had shrieked " No ling-
ering !   Let me be fell ; force I must be brief."

O the mind, mind has mountains ; cliffs of fall
Frightful, sheer, no-man-fathomed. Hold them cheap
May who ne'er hung there. Nor does long our small
Durance deal with that steep or deep. Here ! creep,
Wretch, under a comfort serves in a whirlwind : all
Life death doth end and each day dies with sleep.

Gerard Manley Hopkins.

6. WHEN GREEN BUDS HANG IN THE ELM . . .

WHEN green buds hang in the elm like dust
  And sprinkle the lime like rain,
Forth I wander, forth I must,
  And drink of life again.

Forth I must by hedgerow bower
  To look at the leaves uncurled,
And stand in fields where cuckoo flowers
  Are lying about the world.

A. E. Housman.

7. THE CAT AND THE MOON

THE cat went here and there
  And the moon spun round like a top,
And the nearest kin of the moon,
The creeping cat, looked up.
Black Minnaloushe stared at the moon,
For wander and wail as he would,
The pure cold light in the sky
Troubled his animal blood.

Minnaloushe runs in the grass
Lifting his delicate feet.
Do you dance, Minnaloushe, do you dance ?
When two close kindred meet
What better than call a dance ?
Maybe the moon may learn,
Tired of that courtly fashion,
A new dance turn.

Minnaloushe creeps through the grass
From moonlit place to place.
The sacred moon overhead
Has taken a new phase.
Does Minnaloushe know that his pupils
Will pass from change to change,
And that from round to crescent,
From crescent to round they range ?
Minnaloushe creeps through the grass
Alone, important and wise,
And lifts to the changing moon
His changing eyes.

W. B. Yeats.

8. SAILING TO BYZANTIUM

I

THAT is no country for old men.   The young
    In one another's arms, birds in the trees,
—Those dying generations—at their song,
The salmon-falls, the mackerel-crowded seas,
Fish, flesh, or fowl, commend all summer long
Whatever is begotten, born, and dies.
Caught in that sensual music all neglect
Monuments of unageing intellect.

II

An aged man is but a paltry thing,
A tattered coat upon a stick, unless
Soul clap its hands and sing, and louder sing
For every tatter in its mortal dress,
Nor is there singing school but studying

Monuments of its own magnificence ;
And therefore I have sailed the seas and come
To the holy city of Byzantium.

III

O sages standing in God's holy fire
As in the gold mosaic of a wall,
Come from the holy fire, perne in a gyre,
And be the singing-masters of my soul.
Consume my heart away ; sick with desire
And fastened to a dying animal
It knows not what it is ; and gather me
Into the artifice of eternity.

IV

Once out of nature I shall never take
My bodily form from any natural thing,
But such a form as Grecian goldsmiths make
Of hammered gold and gold enamelling
To keep a drowsy Emperor awake ;
Or set upon a golden bough to sing
To lords and ladies of Byzantium
Of what is past, or passing, or to come.

W. B. Yeats.

9. BYZANTIUM

THE unpurged images of day recede ;
    The Emperor's drunken soldiery are abed ;
Night resonance recedes, night-walkers' song
After great cathedral gong ;
A starlit or a moonlit dome distains

All that man is,
All mere complexities,
The fury and the mire of human veins.

Before me floats an image, man or shade,
Shade more than man, more image than a shade;
For Hades' bobbin bound in mummy-cloth
May unwind the winding path;
A mouth that has no moisture and no breath
Breathless mouths may summon;
I hail the superhuman;
I call it death-in-life and life-in-death.

Miracle, bird or golden handiwork,
More miracle than bird or handiwork,
Planted on the starlit golden bough,
Can like the cocks of Hades crow,
Or, by the moon embittered, scorn aloud
In glory of changeless metal
Common bird or petal
And all complexities of mire or blood.

At midnight on the Emperor's pavement flit
Flames that no faggot feeds, nor steel has lit
Nor storm disturbs, flames begotten of flame,
Where blood-begotten spirits come
And all complexities of fury leave,
Dying into a dance,
An agony of trance,
An agony of flame that cannot singe a sleeve.

Astraddle on the dolphin's mire and blood,
Spirit after spirit ! The smithies break the flood,
The golden smithies of the Emperor !
Marbles of the dancing floor
Break bitter furies of complexity,
Those images that yet
Fresh images beget,
That dolphin-torn, that gong-tormented sea.

W. B. Yeats.

10. A DIALOGUE OF SELF AND SOUL

I

My Soul. I summon to the winding ancient stair ;
Set all your mind upon the steep ascent,
Upon the broken, crumbling battlement,
Upon the breathless starlit air,
Upon the star that marks the hidden pole ;
Fix every wandering thought upon
That quarter where all thought is done :
Who can distinguish darkness from the soul ?

My Self. The consecrated blade upon my knees
Is Sato's ancient blade, still as it was,
Still razor-keen, still like a looking-glass
Unspotted by the centuries ;
That flowering, silken, old embroidery, torn
From some court-lady's dress and round
The wooden scabbard bound and wound,
Can, tattered, still protect, faded adorn.

My Soul.   Why should the imagination of a man
          Long past his prime remember things that are
          Emblematical of love and war ?
          Think of ancestral night that can,
          If but imagination scorn the earth
          And intellect its wandering
          To this and that and t'other thing,
          Deliver from the crime of death and birth.

My Self.   Montashigi, third of his family, fashioned it
          Five hundred years ago, about it lie
          Flowers from I know not what embroidery—
          Heart's purple—and all these I set
          For emblems of the day against the tower
          Emblematical of the night,
          And claim as by a soldier's right
          A charter to commit the crime once more.

My Soul.   Such fullness in that quarter overflows
          And falls into the basin of the mind
          That man is stricken deaf and dumb and blind,
          For intellect no longer knows
          Is from the *Ought,* or *Knower* from the *Known*—
          That is to say, ascends to Heaven ;
          Only the dead can be forgiven ;
          But when I think of that my tongue's a stone.

II

My Self.   A living man is blind and drinks his drop.
          What matter if the ditches are impure ?
          What matter if I live it all once more ?

Endure that toil of growing up ;
The ignominy of boyhood ; the distress
Of boyhood changing into man ;
The unfinished man and his pain
Brought face to face with his own clumsiness ;

The finished man among his enemies ?—
How in the name of Heaven can he escape
That defiling and disfigured shape
The mirror of malicious eyes
Casts upon his eyes until at last
He thinks that shape must be his shape ?
And what's the good of an escape
If honour find him in the wintry blast ?

I am content to live it all again
And yet again, if it be life to pitch
Into the frog-spawn of a blind man's ditch,
A blind man battering blind men ;
Or into that most fecund ditch of all,
The folly that man does
Or must suffer, if he woos
A proud woman not kindred of his soul.

I am content to follow to its source,
Every event in action or in thought ;
Measure the lot ; forgive myself the lot !
When such as I cast out remorse
So great a sweetness flows into the breast
We must laugh and we must sing,

We are blest by everything,
Everything we look upon is blest.

W. B. Yeats.

11. IN THE FIELDS

Lord, when I look at lovely things which pass,
    Under old trees the shadows of young leaves
Dancing to please the wind along the grass,
    Or the gold stillness of the August sun on the August
        sheaves;
Can I believe there is a heavenlier world than this?
    And if there is
Will the strange heart of any everlasting thing
    Bring me these dreams that take my breath away?
They come at evening with the home-flying rooks and
        the scent of hay,
    Over the fields.   They come in Spring.

Charlotte Mew.

12. THE CALL

From our low seat beside the fire
    Where we have dozed and dreamed and watched
        the glow
    Or raked the ashes, stopping so
We scarcely saw the sun or rain
    Above, or looked much higher
Than this same quiet red or burned-out fire.
        To-night we heard a call,
        A rattle on the window-pane,
        A voice on the sharp air,
And felt a breath stirring our hair,

A flame within us : Something swift and tall
Swept in and out and that was all.
Was it a bright or a dark angel ?   Who can know ?
    It left no mark upon the snow,
        But suddenly it snapped the chain
        Unbarred, flung wide the door
        Which will not shut again ;
And so we cannot sit here any more.
        We must arise and go ;
    The world is cold without
    And dark and hedged about
    With mystery and enmity and doubt,
        But we must go
    Though yet we do not know
Who called, or what marks we shall leave upon the
    snow.

Charlotte Mew.

13. THE SONG OF SHADOWS

SWEEP thy faint strings, Musician,
    With thy long lean hand ;
Downward the starry tapers burn,
    Sinks soft the waning sand ;
The old hound whimpers couched in sleep
    The embers smoulder low ;
Across the wall the shadows
    Come, and go.

Sweep softly thy strings, Musician,
    The minutes mount to hours ;

Frost on the windless casement weaves
   A labyrinth of flowers ;
Ghosts linger in the darkening air,
   Hearken at the open door ;
Music hath called them, dreaming,
   Home once more.

Walter de la Mare.

14. THE GHOST

"WHO knocks ? "   " I, who was beautiful,
   Beyond all dreams to restore,
I, from the roots of the dark thorn am hither,
And knock on the door."

" Who speaks ? "   " I—once was my speech
Sweet as the bird's on the air.
When echo lurks by the waters to heed ;
'Tis I speak thee fair."

" Dark is the hour ! "   " Ay, and cold."
" Lone is my house."   " Ah, but mine ? "
" Sight, touch, lips, eyes yearned in vain."
" Long dead these to thine . . ."

Silence.   Still faint on the porch
Brake the flames of the stars.
In gloom groped a hope-wearied hand
Over keys, bolts, and bars.

A face peered.   All the grey night
In chaos of vacancy shone ;
Nought but vast Sorrow was there—
The sweet cheat gone.
Walter de la Mare.

15. THE OWL

DOWNHILL I came, hungry, and yet not starved ;
    Cold, yet had heat within me that was proof
Against the North wind ; tired, yet so that rest
Had seemed the sweetest thing under a roof.

Then at the inn I had food, fire, and rest,
Knowing how hungry, cold, and tired was I.
All of the night was quite barred out except
An owl's cry, a most melancholy cry

Shaken out long and clear upon the hill,
No merry note, nor cause of merriment,
But one telling me plain what I escaped
And others could not, that night, as in I went.

And salted was my food, and my repose,
Salted and sobered, too, by the bird's voice
Speaking for all who lay under the stars,
Soldiers and poor, unable to rejoice.
Edward Thomas.

16. OLD MAN

OLD Man, or Lad's-love,—in the name there's
    nothing
To one that knows not Lad's-love, or Old Man,
The hoar-green feathery herb, almost a tree,

Growing with rosemary and lavender.
Even to one that knows it well, the names
Half decorate, half perplex, the thing it is :
At least, what that is clings not to the names
In spite of time.   And yet I like the names.

The herb itself I like not, but for certain
I love it, as some day the child will love it
Who plucks a feather from the door-side bush
Whenever she goes in or out of the house.
Often she waits there, snipping the tips and shrivelling
The shreds at last on to the path, perhaps
Thinking, perhaps of nothing, till she sniffs
Her fingers and runs off.   The bush is still
But half as tall as she, though it is as old ;
So well she clips it.   Not a word she says ;
And I can only wonder how much hereafter
She will remember, with that bitter scent,
Of garden rows, and ancient damson trees
Topping a hedge, a bent path to a door,
A low thick bush beside the door, and me
Forbidding her to pick.

                              As for myself,
Where first I met the bitter scent is lost.
I, too, often shrivel the grey shreds,
Sniff them and think and sniff again and try
Once more to think what it is I am remembering,
Always in vain.   I cannot like the scent,
Yet I would rather give up others more sweet,
With no meaning, than this bitter one.

I have mislaid the key.   I sniff the spray
And think of nothing ; I see and I hear nothing ;
Yet seem, too, to be listening, lying in wait
For what I should, yet never can, remember :
No garden appears, no path, no hoar-green bush
Of Lad's-love, or Old Man, no child beside,
Neither father nor mother, nor any playmate ;
Only an avenue, dark, nameless, without end.

Edward Thomas.

17. LIGHTS OUT

I HAVE come to the borders of sleep,
  The unfathomable deep
Forest where all must lose
Their way, however straight,
Or winding, soon or late ;
They cannot choose.

Many a road and track
That, since the dawn's first crack,
Up to the forest brink,
Deceived the travellers,
Suddenly now blurs,
And in they sink.

Here love ends,
Despair, ambition ends ;
All pleasure and all trouble,
Although most sweet or bitter,
Here ends in sleep that is sweeter
Than tasks most noble.

There is not any book
Or face of dearest look
That I would not turn from now
To go into the unknown
I must enter and leave alone
I know not how.

The tall forest towers ;
Its cloudy foliage lowers
Ahead, shelf above shelf ;
Its silence I hear and obey
That I may lose my way
And myself.

Edward Thomas.

18. THE UNKNOWN BIRD

THREE lovely notes he whistled, too soft to be heard
    If others sang ; but others never sang
In the great beech-wood all that May and June.
No one saw him : I alone could hear him
Though many listened. Was it but four years
Ago ? or five ? He never came again.

Oftenest when I heard him I was alone,
Nor could I ever make another hear,
La-la-la ! he called seeming far-off—
As if a cock crowed past the edge of the world,
As if the bird or I were in a dream.
Yet that he travelled through the trees and sometimes
Neared me, was plain, though somehow distant still
He sounded. All the proof is—I told men
What I had heard.

     I never knew a voice,
Man, beast, or bird, better than this. I told
The naturalists ; but neither had they heard
Anything like the notes that did so haunt me,
I had them clear by heart and have them still.
Four years, or five, have made no difference. Then
As now that La-la-la ! was bodiless sweet :
Sad more than joyful it was, if I must say
That it was one or other, but if sad
'Twas sad only with joy too, too far off
For me to taste it. But I cannot tell
If truly never anything but fair
The days were when he sang, as now they seem.
This surely I know, that I who listened then,
Happy sometimes, sometimes suffering
A heavy body and a heavy heart,
Now straightway, if I think of it, become
Light as that bird wandering beyond my shore.
         Edward Thomas.

19. the old trouper

i ran onto mehitabel again
 last evening
she is inhabiting
a decayed trunk
which lies in an alley
in greenwich village
in company with the
most villainous tom cat

i have ever seen
but there is nothing
wrong about the association
archy she told me
it is merely a plutonic
attachment
and the thing can be
believed for the tom
looks like one of pluto s demons
it is a theatre trunk
archy mehitabel told me
and tom is an old theatre cat
he has given his life
to the theatre
he claims that richard
mansfield once
kicked him out of the way
and then cried because
he had done it and
petted him
and at another time
he says in a case
of emergency
he played a bloodhound
in a production of
uncle tom s cabin
the stage is not what it
used to be tom says
he puts his front paw
on his breast and says
they don t have it any more

they don t have it here
the old troupers are gone
there s nobody can troupe
any more
they are all amateurs nowadays
they haven t got it
here
there are only
five or six of us oldtime
troupers left
this generation does not know
what stage presence is
personality is what they lack
personality
where would they get
the training my old friends
got in the stock companies
i knew mr booth very well
says tom
and a law should be passed
preventing anybody else
from ever playing
in any play he ever
played in
there was a trouper for you
i used to sit on his knee
and purr when i was
a kitten he used to tell me
how much he valued my opinion
finish is what they lack
finish

and they haven t got it
here
and again he laid his paw
on his breast
i remember mr daly very
well too
i was with mr daly s company
for several years
there was art for you
there was team work
there was direction
they knew the theatre
and they all had it
here
for two years mr daly
would not ring up the curtain
unless i was in the
prompter s box
they are amateurs nowadays
rank amateurs all of them
for two seasons i played
the dog in joseph
jefferson s rip van winkle
it is true i never came
on the stage
but he knew i was just off
and it helped him
i would like to see
one of your modern
theatre cats
act a dog so well

that it would convince
a trouper like jo jefferson
but they haven t got it
nowadays
they haven t got it
here
jo jefferson had it he had it
here
i come of a long line
of theatre cats
my grandfather
was with forrest
he had it he was a real trouper
my grandfather said
he had a voice
that used to shake
the ferryboats
on the north river
once he lost his beard
and my grandfather
dropped from the
fly gallery and landed
under his chin
and played his beard
for the rest of the act
you don t see any theatre
cats that could do that
nowadays
they haven t got it they
haven t got it
here

once i played the owl
in modjeska s production
of macbeth
i sat above the castle gate
in the murder scene
and made my yellow
eyes shine through the dusk
like an owl s eyes
modjeska was a real
trouper she knew how to pick
her support i would like
to see any of these modern
theatre cats play the owl s eyes
to modjeska s lady macbeth
but they haven t got it nowadays
they haven t got it
here

mehitabel he says
both our professions
are being ruined
by amateurs
archy
Don Marquis.

20. GENERAL WILLIAM BOOTH ENTERS INTO HEAVEN

[To be sung to the tune of *The Blood of the Lamb* with indicated instrument]

I

[*Bass drum beaten loudly*]

BOOTH led boldly with his big bass drum—
(Are you washed in the blood of the Lamb?)

The Saints smiled gravely and they said : "He's come."
(Are you washed in the blood of the Lamb ?)
Walking lepers following, rank on rank,
Lurching bravoes from the ditches dank,
Drabs from the alleyways and drug fiends pale—
Minds still passion-ridden, soul-powers frail :—
Vermin-eaten saints with mouldy breath,
Unwashed legions with the ways of Death—
(Are you washed in the blood of the Lamb ?)

[*Banjos.*]

Every slum had sent its half-a-score
The round world over.   (Booth had groaned for more.)
Every banner that the wide world flies
Bloomed with glory and transcendent dyes.
Big-voiced lasses made their banjos bang,
Tranced, fanatical they shrieked and sang :—
" Are you washed in the blood of the Lamb ? "
Hallelujah !   It was queer to see
Bull-necked convicts with that land make free.
Loons with trumpets blowed a blare, blare, blare
On, on upward thro' the golden air !
(Are you washed in the blood of the Lamb ?)

II

[*Bass drum slower and softer.*]

Booth died blind and still by Faith he trod,
Eyes still dazzled by the ways of God.
Booth led boldly and he looked the chief

Eagle countenance in sharp relief,
Beard a-flying, air of high command
Unabated in that holy land.

[*Sweet flute music.*]

Jesus came from out the court-house door,
Stretched his hands above the passing poor.
Booth saw not, but led his queer ones there
Round and round the mighty court-house square.
Yet in an instant all that blear review
Marched on spotless, clad in raiment new.
The lame were straightened, withered limbs uncurled
And blind eyes opened on a new, sweet world.

[*Bass drum louder.*]

Drabs and vixens in a flash made whole !
Gone was the weasel-head, the snout, the jowl !
Sages and sibyls now, and athletes clean,
Rulers of empires, and of forests green !

[*Grand chorus of all instruments.   Tambourines to the
    foreground.*]

The hosts were sandalled, and their wings were fire !
(Are you washed in the blood of the Lamb ?)
But their noise played havoc with the angel-choir.
(Are you washed in the blood of the Lamb ?)
O, shout Salvation !   It was good to see
Kings and Princes by the Lamb set free.
The banjos rattled and the tambourines
Jing-jing-jingled in the hands of Queens.

[*Reverently sung, no instruments.*]
And when Booth halted by the curb for prayer
He saw his Master thro' the flag-filled air.
Christ came gently with a robe and crown
For Booth the soldier, while the throng knelt down.
He saw King Jesus. They were face to face,
And he knelt a-weeping in that holy place.
Are you washed in the blood of the Lamb ?

Vachel Lindsay.

21. CAT'S MEAT

Ho, all you cats in all the street ;
   Look out, it is the hour of meat :

The little barrow is crawling along,
And the meat-boy growling his fleshy song.

Hurry, Ginger ! Hurry, White !
Don't delay to court or fight.

Wandering Tabby, vagrant Black,
Yamble from adventure back !

Slip across the shining street,
Meat ! Meat ! Meat ! Meat !

Lift your tail and dip your feet ;
Find your penny—Meat ! Meat !

Where's your mistress ? Learn to purr :
Pennies emanate from her.

Be to her, for she is Fate,
Perfectly affectionate.

(You, domestic Pinkie-Nose,
Keep inside and warm your toes.)

Flurry, flurry in the street—
Meat ! Meat ! Meat ! Meat !

Harold Monro.

22. CLOCK

WHEN first you learn to read a clock
    That moment you are in a snare,
Doomed for the rest of life to stand
A victim to that patient hand.

The large round eyes of time begin to stare ;
The voice of time,
With tick and tock,
Beats like a heart against your ear.

Now all the clocks form close about,
And from the middle of that ring
You crane to find one passage out
In horror what their time may bring.
And is there no escape outside the circle
Where everything you do is overlooked ?

I'd like to stare them through the eyes,
And see beyond that moony dial :
For backward from the axis of a clock,
Like gossamer at first,
Tight-braced strands, and cords becoming chains,

Lead, climb, and spread themselves away in space ;
So It, their intimate converging place,
Acquires gigantic intricate communions,
Copious relation to forces beyond forces,
(Cool and placid though it look).
Away and away beyond it, range on range,
In all their tortuous elemental courses,
The hidden worlds pursue their time and change ;
Are, and then are no more,
Then are again—while we,
Crouched near their ticking dials, faintly guess,
And, as when listening to a far-off ocean,
Hear more, hear less,
Then often not at all,
And visualize the foamy green commotion
Of the great roaring waves that break and fall.

Harold Monro.

23. REAL PROPERTY

TELL *me about that harvest field.*
   Oh !   Fifty acres of living bread.
The colour has painted itself in my heart.
The form is patterned in my head.

So now I take it everywhere ;
See it whenever I look round ;
Hear it growing through every sound,
Know exactly the sound it makes—
Remembering, as one must all day,
Under the pavement the live earth aches.

Trees are at the farther end,
Limes all full of the mumbling bee :

So there must be a harvest field
Whenever one thinks of a linden tree.

A hedge is about it, very tall,
Hazy and cool, and breathing sweet.
Round paradise is such a wall
And all the day, in such a way,
In paradise the wild birds call.

You only need to close your eyes
And go within your secret mind,
And you'll be into paradise :
I've learnt quite easily to find
Some linden trees and drowsy bees,
A tall sweet hedge with the corn behind.

I will not have that harvest mown :
I'll keep the corn and leave the bread.
I've bought that field ; it's now my own ;
I've fifty acres in my head.
I take it as a dream to bed.
I carry it about all day. . . .

Sometimes when I have found a friend
I give a blade of corn away.

Harold Monro.

24. MAN CARRYING BALE

THE tough hand closes gently on the load ;
　　　Out of the mind, a voice
Calls " Lift ! " and the arms, remembering well their
　　　work,
Lengthen and pause for help.

Then a slow ripple flows along the body,
While all the muscles call to one another :
 " Lift ! " and the bulging bale
 Floats like a butterfly in June.

So moved the earliest carrier of bales,
 And the same watchful sun
Glowed through his body feeding it with light.
 So will the last one move,
And halt, and dip his head, and lay his load
Down, and the muscles will relax and tremble. . . .
 Earth, you designed your man
 Beautiful both in labour, and repose.

Harold Monro.

25. RHYMELESS

You ask a rhymeless sonnet since, you say,
 The world's untuned and discords jar the soul,
And hopes are fallen, purpose fickle ; so
A broken shape is best for poetry
That would our day interpret to itself.
—But what has poetry to do with lies,
Delusions, and the mystery of self-love,
That it should match the misery by its own ?
Poetry is the body given by strong
Imagination to the waste of life,
The wheel on which the perfect bowl is shaped
To hold the ashes of forgotten folk ;
The shell that keeps a heavenly air unbroken,
Words of a tongue that else had died unspoken.

John Freeman.

26. NIGHTFALL
Sanctuary Wood, 1917

HOODED in angry mist, the sun goes down :
    Steel-gray the clouds roll out across the sea :
Is this a Kingdom ?   Then give Death the crown,
For here no emperor hath won, save He.

Herbert Asquith.

27. THE RETURN

SEE, they return ; ah, see the tentative
    Movements, and the slow feet,
The trouble in the pace and the uncertain
Wavering !

See, they return, one, and by one,
With fear, as half-awakened ;
As if the snow should hesitate
And murmur in the wind,
         and half turn back ;
These were the " Wing'd-with-Awe,"
        Inviolable.

Gods of the wingèd shoe !
With them the silver hounds,
        sniffing the trace of air !

Haie ! Haie !
    These were the swift to harry ;
These the keen-scented ;
These were the souls of blood.

Slow on the leash,
       pallid the leash-men !

Ezra Pound.

28. ENVOI (1919)

Go, dumb-born book,
    Tell her that sang me once that song of Lawes :
Hadst thou but song
As thou hast subjects known,
Then were there cause in thee that should condone
Even my faults that heavy upon me lie,
And build her glories their longevity.

Tell her that sheds
Such treasure in the air,
Recking naught else but that her graces give
Life to the moment,
I would bid them live
As roses might, in magic amber laid,
Red overwrought with orange and all made
One substance and one colour
Braving time.

Tell her that goes
With song upon her lips
But sings not out the song, nor knows
The maker of it, some other mouth,
May be as fair as hers,
Might, in new ages, gain her worshippers,
When our two dusts, with Waller's shall be laid,
Siftings on siftings in oblivion,
Till change hath broken down
All things save Beauty alone.

Ezra Pound.

29. KUNG'S WISDOM

(Canto XIII)

Kung walked
      by the dynastic temple
and into the cedar grove,
      and then out by the lower river,
And with him Khieu Tchi
      and Tian the low speaking
And " we are unknown," said Kung,
" You will take up charioteering ?
      " Then you will become known,
" Or perhaps I should take up charioteering, or archery ?
" Or the practice of public speaking ? "
And Tseu-lou said, "I would put the defences in order,"
And Khieu said, " If I were lord of a province
" I would put it in better order than this is."
And Tchi said, " I should prefer a small mountain
                         temple,
" With order in the observances,
      with a suitable performance of the ritual,"
And Tian said, with his hand on the strings of his lute
The low sounds continuing
      after his hand left the strings,
And the sound went up like smoke, under the leaves,
And he looked after the sound :
      " The old swimming hole,
" And the boys flopping off the planks,
" Or sitting in the underbrush playing mandolins."
      And Kung smiled upon all of them equally.

And Theng-sie desired to know :
      " Which had answered correctly ? "
And Kung said, " They have all answered correctly,
" That is to say, each in his nature."
And Kung raised his cane against Yuan Jang,
      Yuan Jang being his elder,
For Yuan Jang sat by the roadside pretending to
    be receiving wisdom.
And Kung said,
      " You old fool, come out of it,
" Get up and do something useful."
      And Kung said,
" Respect a child's faculties
" From the moment it inhales the clear air,
" But a man of fifty who knows nothing
      " Is worthy of no respect."
And " When the prince has gathered about him
" All the savants and artists, his riches will be fully
                    employed."
And Kung said, and wrote on the bo leaves :
      " If a man have not order within him
" He can not spread order about him ;
" And if a man have not order within him
" His family will not act with due order ;
      " And if the prince have not order within him
" He can not put order in his dominions."
And Kung gave the words " order "
and " brotherly deference "
And said nothing of the " life after death ".
And he said,
      " Anyone can run to excesses,

" It is easy to shoot past the mark,
" It is hard to stand firm in the middle."

And they said : " If a man commit murder
     "Should his father protect him, and hide him ? "
And Kung said :
     " He should hide him."

And Kung gave his daughter to Kong-Tchang
     Although Kong-Tchang was in prison.
And he gave his niece to Nan-Young
     although Nan-Young was out of office,
And Kung said " Wang ruled with moderation,
     " In his day the State was well kept,
" And even I can remember
" A day when the historians left blanks in their writings,
" I mean for things they didn't know,
" But that time seems to be passing."
And Kung said, " Without character you will
     be unable to play on that instrument
" Or to execute the music fit for the Odes.
" The blossoms of the apricot
     blow from the east to the west,
" And I have tried to keep them from falling."

Ezra Pound.

30. SPHINX

But why do I feel so strangely about you ?
     Said the lovely young lady, half wistful, half
menacing.

I took to my heels and ran
before she could set the claws of her self-absorbed
                              questioning in me.
or tear me with the fangs of disappointment
because I could not answer the riddle of her own
                              self-importance.
                              D. H. Lawrence.

31. GREEN

THE dawn was apple-green,
     The sky was green wine held up in the sun,
The moon was a golden petal between.

She opened her eyes, and green
They shone, clear like flowers undone
For the first time, now for the first time seen.
                              D. H. Lawrence.

32. WORK

THERE is no point in work
     unless it absorbs you
like an absorbing game.

If it doesn't absorb you
if it's never any fun,
don't do it.

When a man goes out into his work
he is alive like a tree in spring,
he is living, not merely working.

When the Hindus weave thin wool into long, long
    lengths of stuff
with their thin dark hands and their wide dark eyes
    and their still souls absorbed
they are like slender trees putting forth leaves, a long
    white web of living leaf,
the tissue they weave,
and they clothe themselves in white as a tree clothes
    itself in its own foliage.

As with cloth, so with houses, ships, shoes, wagons or
    cups or loaves
men might put them forth as a snail its shell, as a
    bird that leans
its breast against its nest, to make it round,
as the turnip models his round root, as the bush makes
    flowers and gooseberries,
putting them forth, not manufacturing them,
and cities might be as once they were, bowers grown
    out from the busy bodies of people.
And so it will be again, men will smash the machines.

At last, for the sake of clothing himself in his own
    leaf-like cloth
tissued from his life,
and dwelling in his own bowery house, like a beaver's
    nibbled mansion
and drinking from cups that came off his fingers like
    flowers off their five-fold stem,
he will cancel the machines we have got.

D. H. Lawrence.

33. MOUNTAIN LION

CLIMBING through the January snow, into the Lobo
canyon
Dark grow the spruce-trees, blue is the balsam, water
sounds still unfrozen, and the trail is still evident.

Men !
Two men !
Men !   The only animal in the world to fear !

They hesitate.
We hesitate.
They have a gun.
We have no gun.

Then we all advance, to meet.

Two Mexicans, strangers, emerging out of the dark
and snow and inwardness of the Lobo valley.
What are they doing here on this vanishing trail ?

What is he carrying ?
Something yellow.
A deer ?

¿ Qué tiene, amigo
León ?
He smiles, foolishly, as if he were caught doing wrong.
And we smile, foolishly, as if we didn't know.
He is quite gentle and dark-faced.

It is a mountain lion,
A long, long slim cat, yellow like a lioness.
Dead.
He trapped her this morning, he says, smiling foolishly.

Lift up her face,
Her round, bright face, bright as frost,
Her round, fine-fashioned head, with two dead ears ;
And stripes in the brilliant frost of her face, sharp,
     fine dark rays,
Dark, keen, fine rays in the brilliant frost of her face.
Beautiful dead eyes.

Hermoso es !

They go out towards the open ;
We go on into the gloom of Lobo.
And above the trees I found her lair,
A hole in the blood-orange brilliant rocks that stick up,
        a little cave.
And bones, and twigs, and a perilous ascent.

So, she will never leap up that way again, with the
        yellow flash of a mountain lion's long shoot !
And her bright striped frost-face will never watch any
        more, out of the shadow of the cave in the blood-
        orange rock,
Above the trees of the Lobo dark valley-mouth !

Instead, I look out.

And out to the dim of the desert, like a dream, never
    real ;
To the snow of the Sangre de Cristo mountains, the
    ice of the mountains of Picoris,
And near across at the opposite steep of snow, green
    trees motionless standing in snow, like a Christmas
    toy.
And I think in this empty world there was room for
    me and a mountain lion.
And I think in the world beyond, how easily we
    might spare a million or two of humans
And never miss them.
Yet what a gap in the world, the missing white frost-
    face of that slim yellow mountain lion !

D. H. Lawrence.

34. BARE ALMOND TREES

WET almond-trees, in the rain,
    Like iron sticking grimly out of earth ;
Black almond trunks, in the rain,
Like iron implements, twisted, hideous, out of the
    earth,
Out of the deep, soft fledge of Sicilian winter-green,
Earth-grass uneatable,
Almond trunks curving blackly, iron-dark, climbing
    the slopes.

Almond-tree, beneath the terrace rail,
Black, rusted, iron trunk,
You have welded your thin stems finer,
Like steel, like sensitive steel in the air,

M.P.—2*

Grey, lavender, sensitive steel, curving thinly and
    brittly up in a parabola.

What are you doing in the December rain ?
Have you a strange electric sensitiveness in your steel
    tips ?
Do you feel the air for electric influences
Like some strange magnetic apparatus ?
Do you take in messages, in some strange code,
From heaven's wolfish, wandering electricity, that
    prowls so constantly round Etna ?
Do you take the whisper of sulphur from the air ?
Do you hear the chemical accents of the sun ?
Do you telephone the roar of the waters over the
    earth ?
And from all this, do you make calculations ?
Sicily, December's Sicily in a mass of rain
With iron branching blackly, rusted like old, twisted
    implements
And brandishing and stooping over earth's wintry
    fledge, climbing the slopes
Of uneatable soft green !

D. H. Lawrence.

35. ON AUGUST THIRTEENTH, AT THE MOUNT, MARSDEN, BUCKS

Out of this seemliness, this solid order,
    At half-past four to-day,
When down below
Geraniums were bright
In the contented glow,

And Jones was planting seedlings all about,
Supremely,
Geometrically right
For all to see
In your herbaceous border,
You had to go,
Who always liked to stay.
Before Louisa sliced the currant roll,
And re-arranged the zinnias in the bowl,
All in a rhythm reachless by modernity,
Correct and slow,
And brought the tea
And tray,
At half-past four on Friday you went out :
To the unseemly, seemly,
Dateless, whole
Light of Eternity
You went away.

Frances Cornford.

36. GRAND BALLET

I SAW you dance that summer before the war.
   Onc thunderous night it was, at Covent Garden,
When we, who walked, beneath the weighted trees,
Hot metropolitan pavements, might have smelt
Blood in the dust, and heard the traffic's cry
Ceaseless and savage like a prophecy.

As by a sunrise sea I saw you stand,
Your sylphides round you on the timeless strand,

White, pure, delicious poisèd butterflies,
The early nineteenth century in their eyes,
And Chopin ready for their silver toes.
(O sighs unsatisfied, and one red rose !)

The fountain of all movement ready to flow
Seemed prisoned in your entrancèd body.   So
You stood, their Prince, most elegantly fair,
Swan-sleeved, black-jacketed, with falling hair
And hands half-raised in ravishment.   O there,
You Grecian arrow fitted to the bow,
You beech-tree in a legendary wood,
You panther in a velvet bolero,
There you for one immortal moment stood—

One moment like a wave before it flows,
Frozen in perfectness.   Then one hand rose
And tossed a silver curl, demurely light
(O grace, O rose, O Chopin and all delight),
And the enchantment broke.
                              That thunderous night
We saw Nijinsky dance.
                              Thereafter fell
On the awaiting world the powers of Hell,
Chaos, and irremediable pain ;
And utter darkness on your empty brain,
Not even grief to say, No more, no more.

But tell me, when my mortal memories wane
As death draws near, and peace is mine and pardon,

Where will it like an escapèd dove repair ?
To what Platonic happy heaven—where ?—where ?—
Untouchable by Fate and free of Time,
That one immortal moment of the mime
We saw Nijinsky dance at Covent Garden ?

Frances Cornford.

37. CHANCE MEETING

TAKE from me something,
    be it all too fine
and untranslatable and worthless
for your purpose,
take it,
it's mine ;
no one can give as I give,
none can say,
" take bountifully and smile
and go away,
then, hate for ever ;
do not stoop to send
the little missive
that might slay or end
this pain for ever."

Your one word might stay
the pain ;
but do not send it ;
keep yourself out of it,
intransient ;
finish what you have begun,

write swiftly
with a stylus
dipped in sun
and tears
and blood,
rain,
hail
and snow ;
dip stylus in the beauty of the translatable
 things you know ;
the things I have
are nameless,
old and true ;
they may not be named ;
few may live and know.

H. D.

38. I WOULD FORGO . . .

I WOULD forgo
 my snowfields for your sun,
I would surrender
crocus
and ice-gentian
and all the lilies
rising one by one,
one after one,
and then another one
like star that flames white fire
to star
as beacon ;

I would forget
the holy marjoram
and all the little speedwells
and low thrift
for just one grain
of your enchantment ; lift
the veil,
dividing me from me,
and heal the scar
my searing helmet made,
and lure me forth
radiant,
unafraid
as the immortals ;

we near heaven's hills with this,
God's asphodels ;
O stay,
stay close,
bend down ;
bend down my dream, my Morpheus,
breathe my soul
straight into you ;
I would revive the whole
of Ilium
and in sacred trance,
show Helen
who made Troy
a barren town.

H. D.

39.   O VIRTUOUS LIGHT

A PRIVATE madness has prevailed
    Over the pure and valiant mind ;
The instrument of reason failed
And the star-gazing eyes struck blind.

Sudden excess of light has wrought
Confusion in the secret place
Where the slow miracles of thought
Take shape through patience into grace.

Mysterious as steel and flint
The birth of this destructive spark
Whose inward growth has power to print
Strange suns upon the natural dark.

O break the walls of sense in half
And make the spirit fugitive !
This light begotten of itself
Is not a light by which to live !

The fire of farthing tallow dips
Dispels the menace of the skies
So it illuminate the lips
And enter the discerning eyes

O virtuous light, if thou be man's
Or matter of the meteor stone,
Prevail against this radiance
Which is engendered of its own !

Elinor Wylie.

40. THE RIDERS

At the dead centre of the boundless plain
        Does our way end ?   Our horses pace and pace
Like steeds for ever labouring on a shield,
Keeping their solitary heraldic courses.

Our horses move on such a ground, for them
Perhaps the progress is all ease and pleasure,
But it is heavy work for us, the riders,
Whose hearts have flown so far ahead they are lost
        Long past all finding
While we sit staring at the same horizon.

Time has such curious stretches, we are told,
And generation after generation
May travel them, sad stationary journey,
Of what device, what meaning ?

                                Yet these coursers
Have seen all and will see all.   Suppliantly
The rocks will melt, the sealed horizons fall
Before their onset—and the places
Our hearts have hid in will be viewed by strangers
Sitting where we are, breathing the foreign air
Of the new realm they have inherited.

But we shall fall here on the plain.

                                It may be
These steeds would stumble and the long road end
(So legend says) if they should lack their riders.

        But then a rider
Is always easy to find.   Yet we fill a saddle
At least.   We sit where others have sat before us
And others will sit after us.

                        It cannot be
These animals know their riders, mark the change
When one makes way for another.   It cannot be
They know this wintry wilderness from spring.
For they have come from regions dreadful past
All knowledge.   They have borne upon their saddles
Forms fiercer than the tiger, borne them calmly
As they bear us now.

                        And so we do not hope
That their great coal-black glossy hides
Should keep a glimmer of the autumn light
We still remember, when our limbs were weightless
As red leaves on a tree, and our silvery breaths
Went on before us like new-risen souls
Leading our empty bodies through the air.
A princely dream.   Now all that golden country
Is razed as bare as Troy.   We cannot return,
And shall not see the kingdom of our heirs.

These beasts are mortal, and we who fall so lightly,
Fall so heavily, are, it is said, immortal.
Such knowledge should armour us against all change,
And this monotony.   Yet these worn saddles
Have powers to charm us to obliviousness.

They were appointed for us, and the scent of the
    ancient leather
Is strong as a spell. So we must mourn or rejoice
For this our station, our inheritance'
As if it were all. This plain all. This journey all.
                        Edwin Muir.

41. THE LITTLE GHOST WHO DIED FOR LOVE

Deborah Churchill, born in 1678, was hanged in 1708 for shielding
her lover in a duel. His opponent was killed, her lover fled to
Holland, and she was killed in his stead, according to the law of
the time. The chronicle said, "Though she died at peace with
God, this malefactor could never understand the justice of her
sentence, to the last moment of her life."

"FEAR not, O maidens, shivering
    As bunches of the dew-drenched leaves
In the calm moonlight . . . it is the cold sends
    quivering
My voice, a little nightingale that grieves.

Now Time beats not, and dead Love is forgotten . . .
The spirit too is dead and dank and rotten,

And I forget the moment when I ran
Between my lover and the sworded man—
Blinded with terror lest I lose his heart.
The sworded man dropped, and I saw depart

Love and my lover and my life . . . he fled
And I was strung and hung upon the tree.
It is so cold now that my heart is dead
And drops through time . . . night is too dark to see

Him still. . . . But it is spring ; upon the fruit-
    boughs of your lips,
Young maids, the dew like India's splendour drips ;
Pass by among the strawberry beds, and pluck the
    berries
Cooled by the silver moon ; pluck boughs of cherries

That seem the lovely lucent coral bough
(From streams of starry milk those branches grow)
That Cassiopeia feeds with her faint light,
Like Ethiopia ever jewelled bright.

Those lovely cherries do enclose
Deep in their sweet hearts the silver snows.

And the small budding flowers upon the trees
Are filled with sweetness like the bags of bees.

Forget my fate . . . but I, a moonlight ghost,
Creep down the strawberry paths and seek the lost

World, the apothecary at the Fair.
I, Deborah, in my long cloak of brown
Like the small nightingale that dances down
The cherried boughs, creep to the doctor's bare
Booth . . . cold as ivy in the air,

And, where I stand, the brown and ragged light
Holds something still beyond, hid from my sight.

Once, plumaged like the sea, his swanskin head

Had wintry white quills . . . 'Hearken to the
  Dead . . .
I was a nightingale, but now I croak
Like some dark harpy hidden in night's cloak,
Upon the walls ; among the Dead, am quick ;
Oh, give me medicine, for the world is sick ;
Not medicines, planet-spotted like fritillaries
For country sins and old stupidities,
Nor potions you may give a country maid
When she is lovesick . . . love in earth is laid,
Grown dead and rotten ' . . . so I sank me down,
Poor Deborah in my long cloak of brown.
Though cockcrow marches, crying of false dawns,
Shall bury my dark voice, yet still it mourns
Among the ruins,—for it is not I
But this old world, is sick and soon must die !"

Edith Sitwell.

42. CRITICS AND CONNOISSEURS

THERE is a great amount of poetry in unconscious
  fastidiousness. Certain Ming
    products, imperial floor-coverings of coach-
  wheel yellow, are well enough in their way but I
                              have seen
        something
      that I like better—a
        mere childish attempt to make an imper-
          fectly ballasted animal stand up,
        similar determination to make a pup
          eat his meat from the plate.

I remember a swan under the willows in Oxford,
     with flamingo-coloured, maple-
        leaflike feet. It reconnoitred like a battle-
ship. Disbelief and conscious fastidiousness were the
     staple ingredients in its
        disinclination to move. Finally its hardihood
           was not proof against its
        proclivity to more fully appraise such bits
           of food as the stream

bore counter to it ; it made away with what I gave it
     to eat. I have seen this swan and
        I have seen you ; I have seen ambition without
understanding in a variety of forms. Happening
                                             to stand
        by an ant-hill, I have
        seen a fastidious ant carrying a stick north,
           south, east, west, till it turned on
        itself, struck out from the flower-bed into the
                                             lawn,
     and returned to the point

from which it had started. Then abandoning the
                                          stick as
        useless and overtaxing its
           jaws with a particle of whitewash—pill-like but
heavy, it again went through the same course of
                                          procedure.
     What is

    there in being able
        to say that one has dominated the stream
                            in an attitude
    of self-defence ;
    in proving that one has had the experience
        of carrying a stick ?

                            Marianne Moore.

43. SILENCE

My father used to say,
    " Superior people never make long visits,
have to be shown Longfellow's grave
or the glass flowers at Harvard.
Self-reliant like the cat—
that takes its prey to privacy,
the mouse's limp tail hanging like a shoelace from its
                            mouth—
they sometimes enjoy solitude,
and can be robbed of speech
by speech which has delighted them.
The deepest feeling always shows itself in silence ;
not in silence, but restraint."
Nor was he insincere in saying, " Make my house
                            your inn."

Inns are not residences.
                            Marianne Moore.

44. THE HOLLOW MEN

A penny for the Old Guy

I

WE are the hollow men
    We are the stuffed men
Leaning together
Headpiece filled with straw. Alas !
Our dried voices, when
We whisper together
Are quiet and meaningless
As wind in dry grass
Or rats' feet over broken glass
In our dry cellar

Shape without form, shade without colour,
Paralysed force, gesture without motion ;

Those who have crossed
With direct eyes, to death's other Kingdom
Remember us—if at all—not as lost
Violent souls, but only
As the hollow men
The stuffed men.

II

Eyes I dare not meet in dreams
In death's dream kingdom
These do not appear :
There, the eyes are

Sunlight on a broken column
There, is a tree swinging
And voices are
In the wind's singing
More distant and more solemn
Than a fading star.

Let me be no nearer
In death's dream kingdom
Let me also wear
Such deliberate disguises
Rat's coat, crowskin, crossed staves
In a field
Behaving as the wind behaves
No nearer—

Not that final meeting
In the twilight kingdom

III

This is the dead land
This is cactus land
Here the stone images
Are raised, here they receive
The supplication of a dead man's hand
Under the twinkle of a fading star.

Is it like this
In death's other kingdom
Waking alone

At the hour when we are
Trembling with tenderness
Lips that would kiss
Form prayers to broken stone.

IV

The eyes are not here
There are no eyes here
In this valley of dying stars
In this hollow valley
This broken jaw of our lost kingdoms

In this last of meeting places
We grope together
And avoid speech
Gathered on this beach of the tumid river

Sightless, unless
The eyes reappear
As the perpetual star
Multifoliate rose
Of death's twilight kingdom
The hope only
Of empty men.

V

Here we go round the prickly pear
Prickly pear prickly pear
Here we go round the prickly pear
At five o'clock in the morning.

Between the idea
And the reality
Between the motion
And the act
Falls the Shadow
                    For Thine is the Kingdom
Between the conception
And the creation
Between the emotion
And the response
Falls the Shadow
                              Life is very long

Between the desire
And the spasm
Between the potency
And the existence
Between the essence
And the descent
Falls the Shadow
                    For Thine is the Kingdom
For Thine is
Life is
For Thine is the

This is the way the world ends
This is the way the world ends
This is the way the world ends
Not with a bang but a whimper.
                              T. S. Eliot.

45. MARINA

Quis hic locus, quae
regio, quae mundi plaga ?

WHAT seas what shores what grey rocks and what
    islands
What water lapping the bow
And scent of pine and the woodthrush singing through
    the fog
What images return
O my daughter.

Those who sharpen the tooth of the dog, meaning
Death
Those who glitter with the glory of the hummingbird,
    meaning
Death
Those who sit in the stye of contentment, meaning
Death
Those who suffer the ecstasy of the animals, meaning
Death

Are become unsubstantial, reduced by a wind,
A breath of pine, and the woodsong fog
By this grace dissolved in place

What is this face, less clear and clearer
The pulse in the arm, less strong and stronger—
Given or lent ? more distant than stars and nearer
    than the eye

Whispers and small laughter between leaves and
    hurrying feet
Under sleep, where all the waters meet.
Bowsprit cracked with ice and paint cracked with heat.
I made this, I have forgotten
And remember.
The rigging weak and the canvas rotten
Between one June and another September.
Made this unknowing, half conscious, unknown, my
    own.
The garboard strake leaks, the seams need caulking.
This form, this face, this life
Living to live in a world of time beyond me ; let me
Resign my life for this life, my speech for that un-
    spoken,
The awakened, lips parted, the hope, the new ships.

What seas what shores what granite islands towards my
    timbers
And woodthrush calling through the fog
My daughter.

T. S. Eliot.

46. THE SOUL OF MAN MUST QUICKEN ..

THE soul of man must quicken to creation.
    Out of the formless stone, when the artist
    unites himself with stone,
Spring always new forms of life, from the soul of man
    that is joined to the soul of stone ;
Out of the meaningless practical shapes of all that is
    living or lifeless

Joined with the artist's eye, new life, new form, new
    colour.
Out of the sea of sound the life of music,
Out of the slimy mud of words, out of the sleet and hail
    of verbal imprecisions,
Approximate thoughts and feelings, words that have
    taken the place of thoughts and feelings,
There spring the perfect order of speech, and the
    beauty of incantation.

T. S. Eliot.

47. WRESTLING

CAME threshing-time, the height of all our seasons.
    We kept the thresher thundering by daylight
And rested all the sweeter after dark
With telling of tales, and washing in the river.
And one there was, some twenty miles a stranger,
Who boasted that he was a mighty wrestler,
And had not met the valiant pair of shoulders
That he could not put down.

We had a champion there. He looked and listened,
He measured off his man, and made his mind up,
And thus he brought great honour to his county :
" My friend, I've heard you bragging, heard you bray-
                            ing,
And now I say for God's sake come and wrestle."
And thus appealed, the other came, for God's sake,
And then they wrestled.

They sprang, they gripped, they strained and rocked
                                  and twisted,
They pounded much good sod to dust and powder,
They ripped the garments off each other vainly
And showed us many naked bulging muscles,
And still were equal.

But while the tide of battle ran so equal,
I heard a sound, I took it for a voice,
I almost saw it spitting out a passage
Between the haggard jaws of my poor hero,
The voice as of a man almost despairing,
With one hope trying when all hopes had failed :
" By God, I'll have you down in one more minute ! "
And it was as he said, for in a minute
He had him down, by God.

John Crowe Ransom.

48. SOUTHERN MANSION

As an intruder I trudged with careful innocence
    To mask decently a quite meddlesome stare,
Passing the old house often on its eminence,
Exhaling my foreign weed on its weighted air.

Here age seemed newly imaged for the historian
After his monstrous châteaux on the Loire ;—
A beauty not for depicting by old vulgarian
Reiterations which gentle readers abhor.

Each time of seeing I absorbed some other feature
Of a house whose legend could in no wise be brief

Nor ignoble.   For it expired as sweetly as Nature,
With her tinge of oxidation on autumn leaf . . .

Stability was the character of its rectangle
Whose line was seen in part and guessed in part
Through trees.   Decay was the note of old brick and
                                        shingle.
Green blinds dragging frightened the watchful heart . . .

At last with my happier angel's own temerity
Did I clang their brazen knocker against the door
To beg their dole of a look, in simple charity,
Or crumbs of history dropping from their full store . . .

The old mistress was ill, and sent my dismissal
By one even more wrappered and lean and dark
Than that warped concierge and imperturbable vassal
Who bids you begone from her master's Gothic park.

Emphatically, the old house crumbled.   The ruins
Would litter, as already the leaves, this petted sward,
And no annalist went in to the lord or the peons ;
The antiquary would gather the bits of shard.

But on retreating, I saw myself in the token
How loving from my Russian weed the feather curled
On the languid air ; and I went with courage shaken
To dip, alas, into some unseemlier world.

                                John Crowe Ransom.

49. BREAK OF DAY IN THE TRENCHES

THE darkness crumbles away—
    It is the same old druid Time as ever.
Only a live thing leaps my hand—
A queer sardonic rat—
As I pull the parapet's poppy
To stick behind my ear.
Droll rat, they would shoot you if they knew
Your cosmopolitan sympathies.
(And God knows what antipathies.)
Now you have touched this English hand
You will do the same to a German—
Soon, no doubt, if it be your pleasure
To cross the sleeping green between.
It seems you inwardly grin as you pass
Strong eyes, fine limbs, haughty athletes
Less chanced than you for life,
Bonds to the whims of murder,
Sprawled in the bowels of the earth,
The torn fields of France.
What do you see in our eyes
At the shrieking iron and flame
Hurled through still heavens ?
What quaver—what heart aghast ?
Poppies whose roots are in man's veins
Drop, and are ever dropping ;
But mine in my ear is safe,
Just a little white with the dust.

Isaac Rosenberg.

50. ON THE COAST OF COROMANDEL

ON the coast of Coromandel
        Dance they to the tunes of Handel;
Chorally, that coral coast
Correlates the bone to ghost,
Till word and limb and note seem one,
Blending, binding act to tone.

All day long they point the sandal
On the coast of Coromandel.
Lemon-yellow legs all bare
Pirouette to peruqued air
From the first green shoots of morn,
Cool as northern hunting-horn,
Till the nightly tropic wind
With its rough-tongued, grating rind
Shatters the frail spires of spice.
Imaged in the lawns of rice
(Mirror-flat and mirror green
Is that lovely water's sheen)
Saraband and rigadoon
Dance they through the purring noon,
While the lacquered waves expand
Golden dragons on the sand—
Dragons that must, steaming, die
From the hot sun's agony—
When elephants, of royal blood,
Plod to bed through lilied mud,
Then evening, sweet as any mango,
Bids them do a gay fandango,

Minuet, jig or gavotte,
How they hate the turkey-trot,
The nautch-dance and the highland fling,
Just as they will never sing
Any music save by Handel
On the coast of Coromandel !

Osbert Sitwell.

51. THE MANNER

Allow no personality to stamp
    Its wayward lines upon your talk or dress ;
Smooth out your facial furrows, on them clamp
The necessary look of nothingness.

You must acquire a careful conversation,
Remember that War-horses of True Breed
Only feel interest—if ever—in relation
To other ones—and never, never read !

Know, though, the names of authors, and conceivably
The names of their most fashionable book ;
But never talk too far, or irretrievably
You blunder on the crafty fisher's hook.

Then music, as a rule, you love too well
To wish to hear.   But if you go, you walk
About—if not too loud, it helps to swell
The frankly social impulse toward talk.

You *simply love* the Opera, and force
Your way in late, and romp from cage to cage ;

The prima-donna is a well-known War-horse
Who fills the heart, the ear, the house, the stage !

If you see modern pictures, in their glass
Ecstatically examine the old strife
Between your food and figure—should he pass,
Discuss with friends the painter's private life.

Though, safety-first, you find it really best
To cast your raptures on the gilded air,
When you find pictures dead, but smartly drest,
Within the mansion of a millionaire.

Still you encourage those whom you can hire
To fix on canvas, for the future race
Of War-horses to simper at—admire,
The painted image of your painted face.

And any artist, author, or musician,
—If second-rate—is useful as a bait
To fish for guests—remember words like " Titian "
"—Shakespeare " "—Mozart," let go—and trust to
    Fate

To pull you through. Avoid ideas—they're common
And might crack through the varnish of your smile,
Impinge upon your worship of God Mammon
Filling your soul with pity, and things vile.

Osbert Sitwell.

52. THE GREATER CATS . . .

THE greater cats with golden eyes
    Stare out between the bars.
Deserts are there, and different skies,
And night with different stars.
They prowl the aromatic hill,
And mate as fiercely as they kill,
And hold the freedom of their will
To roam, to live, to drink their fill ;
But this beyond their wit know I :
Man loves a little, and for long shall die.

Their kind across the desert range
Where tulips spring from stones,
Not knowing they will suffer change
Or vultures pick their bones.
Their strength's eternal in their sight,
They rule the terror of the night,
They overtake the deer in flight,
And in their arrogance they smite ;
But I am sage, if they are strong :
Man's love is transient as his death is long.

Yet oh what powers to deceive !
My wit is turned to faith,
And at this moment I believe
In love, and scout at death,
I came from nowhere and shall be
Strong, steadfast, swift, eternally :
I am a lion, a stone, a tree,

And as the Polar star in me
Is fixed my constant heart on thee.
Ah, may I stay forever blind
With lions, tigers, leopards, and their kind.
Victoria Sackville-West.

53. THE LAND
(Spring)

WHO has not seen the spring, is blind, is dead.
    Better for him that he should coffined lie,
And in that coin his toll to Nature pay
That live a debtor.   All things shall pass by
That fret his mind : the shift of policy,
Princes' ambition, wiser governance,
Civilisation's tides.   There's dissonance
By our great necessary Babel bred,
Perplexes eager spirits unprepared,
Puts out their seeing eyes, leaves their blind touch
To grope past prejudice and ignorance
Towards solution, as they throw away
Each broken, each successive crutch.
Such truths as we have snared
Into the spread conspiracy of our nets,
Come to us fragmentary from a whole,
As meteorites from space.   Now science sets
Two splintered ends together, makes one shred
Corroborate another ; now live flesh
Persuades us by its drunken fallacy ;
Now the instinctive soul
Takes its short-cut to grace ; now blown by gust
Of hazard, truth's entangled in strange mesh,
Else how should poetry,

The runes of divination, superstition
Fastening sharp claw on common circumstance,
Even artifice as neat astrology
Twisting the very stars to fit man's ends,
Mingle some ore with dross of sorcery
Unless the fragment of the whole be part ?
There's some relation we may not adjust,
Some concord of creation that the mind
Only in perilous balance apprehends,
Loth, fugitive, obscure.
All else dies in its season ; all perplexities,
Even human grief with human body dies,
Such griefs that press so wildly on the heart
As to crush in its shell.   But still endure
Nature's renewal and man's fortitude,
A common thing, a permanent common thing,
So coarse, so stated, usual, and so rude,
So quiet in performance, and so slow
That hurrying wit outruns it.   Yet with spring
Life leaps ; her fountains flow ;
And nimble foolish wit must humbled go.

Victoria Sackville-West.

54. FUTILITY

Move him into the sun—
    Gently its touch awoke him once,
At home, whispering of fields unsown.
Always it woke him, even in France,
Until this morning and this snow.
If anything might rouse him now
The kind old sun will know.

Think how it wakes the seeds,—
Woke, once, the clays of a cold star.
Are limbs, so dear-achieved, are sides,
Full-nerved—still warm—too hard to stir ?
Was it for this the clay grew tall ?
—O what made fatuous sunbeams toil
To break earth's sleep at all ?

Wilfred Owen.

55. STRANGE MEETING

IT seemed that out of battle I escaped
   Down some profound dull tunnel, long since
     scooped
Through granites which titanic wars had groined.
Yet also there encumbered sleepers groaned,
Too fast in thought or death to be bestirred.
Then, as I probed them, one sprang up, and stared
With piteous recognition in fixed eyes,
Lifting distressful hands as if to bless.
And by his smile, I knew that sullen hall,
By his dead smile I knew we stood in Hell.
With a thousand pains that vision's face was grained ;
Yet no blood reached there from the upper ground,
And no guns thumped, or down the flues made moan.
" Strange friend," I said, " here is no cause to mourn."
" None," said the other, " save the undone years,
The hopelessness. Whatever hope is yours,
Was my life also ; I went hunting wild
After the wildest beauty in the world.

Which lies not calm in eyes, or braided hair,
But mocks the steady running of the hour,
And if it grieves, grieves richlier than here.
For by my glee might many men have laughed,
And of my weeping something had been left,
Which must die now.   I mean the truth untold,
The pity of war, the pity war distilled.
Now men will go content with what we spoiled.
Or, discontent, boil bloody, and be spilled.
They will be swift with swiftness of the tigress,
None will break ranks, though nations trek from pro-
        gress.
Courage was mine, and I had mystery,
Wisdom was mine, and I had mastery ;
To miss the march of this retreating world
Into vain citadels that are not walled.
Then, when much blood had clogged their chariot-
        wheels
I would go up and wash them from sweet wells,
Even with truths that lie too deep for taint.
I would have poured my spirit without stint
But not through wounds ; not on the cess of war.
Foreheads of men have bled where no wounds were.
I am the enemy you killed, my friend.
I knew you in this dark ; for so you frowned
Yesterday through me as you jabbed and killed.
I parried ; but my hands were loath and cold.
Let us sleep now. . . ."

                              Wilfred Owen.

56. MUD

Twenty years ago
    My generation learned
To be afraid of mud.
We watched its vileness grow,
Deeper and deeper churned
From earth, spirit, and blood.

From earth, sweet-smelling enough
As moorland, field, and coast ;
Firm beneath the corn,
Noble to the plough ;
Purified by frost
Every winter morn.

From blood, the invisible river
Pulsing from the hearts
Of patient man and beast :
The healer and life-giver ;
The union of parts ;
The meaning of the feast.

From spirit, which is man
In triumphant mood,
Conqueror of fears,
Alchemist of pain
Changing bad to good ;
Master of the Spheres.

Earth the king of space,
Blood, the king of time,

Spirit, their lord and god,
All tumbled from their place,
All trodden into slime,
All mingled into mud.

Richard Church.

57. SECRET SERVICE

HERE at the inn, become anonymous !
  No longer the familiar bunch of keys
Burdens my pocket. I have turned the locks,
Left the doors wide for those who care to search
In the old place, the lifetime lair.

                              Farewell
To habit and to name. I am called Pilgrim,
And travel is my habit. I am restless,
Rootless, have surrendered my five senses,
And the possession of love, the confidence
Of marriage. I am like the Jew, the sailor;
The man of service, the ever-questing man.

I have broken old bonds, sworn a new vow
To acknowledge no vow, to accept no duty.
My flight is irresponsible, I am free.
" Who are you ? " asks the stranger at the inn,
The voice in the new city, voice on the road,
The wondering, wandering voice in the air I breathe,
The voice over the ruins of my old self, my world
That quaked and is broken, the world lying open
With the keys in the locks, and the doors flung **wide.**

" I am the guest," I answer at the inn,
" The guest for a night. I am the rootless **man.**

I am the man without child, the man who has left
The pillow, the bosom, the protective arms
And the regenerative sleep at night.
I am the man with a ticket, a summons to go.
My place is in the corridors of life,
And I shall know for my caress, the wind
At the corners of the world. Ever unknown,
Man of no service, man of no secrets, the man
Murdered one night at the inn, the anonymous man."

Richard Church.

58. FOUR III

here's a little mouse) and
what does he think about, i
wonder as over this
floor (quietly with
bright eyes) drifts (nobody
can tell because
Nobody knows, or why
jerks Here &, here,
gr(oo)ving the room's Silence) this like
a littlest
poem a
(with wee ears and see ?
tail frisks)
      (gonE)
" mouse,"
      We are not the same you and
i, since here's a little he

or is
it It
? (or was something we saw in the mirror)?

therefore we'll kiss ; for maybe
what was Disappeared
into ourselves
who (look).   , startled

E. E. Cummings.

59. THE RIVER

THE gravel shone with streaks of gold
  Under the golden light of day :
The summer air no more than trembled
And all the minnows ran away.

To still the beating of their hearts
They gathered in a great platoon.
" What blew so thunderous ? " they said :
" Is the Last Judgment here so soon ? "

One took his courage in both hands
And crept out on a bold campaign :
The shadow of a starling fell,
And how he bolted back again !

Alan Porter.

60. LARK DESCENDING

A SINGING firework ; the sun's darling ;
  Hark how creation pleads !
Then silence : see, a small grey bird
  That runs among the weeds.

Edmund Blunden.

61.　IN BROKEN IMAGES

HE is quick, thinking in clear images ;
　　I am slow, thinking in broken images.

He becomes dull, trusting to his clear images ;
I become sharp, mistrusting my broken images.

Trusting his images, he assumes their relevance ;
Mistrusting my images, I question their relevance.

Assuming their relevance, he assumes the fact,
Questioning their relevance, I question the fact.

When the fact fails him, he questions his senses ;
When the fact fails me, I approve my senses.

He continues quick and dull in his clear images ;
I continue slow and sharp in my broken images.

He in a new confusion of his understanding ;
I in a new understanding of my confusion.

Robert Graves.

62.　TIME

THE vague sea thuds against the marble cliffs
　　And from their fragments age-long grinds
Pebbles like flowers.

Or the vague weather wanders in the fields,
When up spring flowers with coloured buds
Like marble pebbles.

The beauty of the flowers is Time, death-grieved ;
The pebbles' beauty too is Time,
Life-weary.

It is all too easy to admire a flower
Or a smooth pebble flower-like freaked
By Time and vagueness.

Time is Time's ease and the sweet oil that coaxes
All obstinate locks and rusty hinges
To loving-kindness.

What monster's proof against that lovesome pair,
Old age and childhood, seals of Time,
His sorrowful vagueness ?

Or will not render him the accustomed thanks :
Humouring age with filial flowers,
Childhood with pebbles ?

Robert Graves.

63. THE LEGS

THERE was this road,
    And it led up-hill,
And it led down-hill,
And round and in and out.

And the traffic was legs,
Legs from the knees down,
Coming and going,
Never pausing.

And the gutters gurgled
With the rain's overflow,
And the sticks on the pavement
Blindly tapped and tapped.

What drew the legs along
Was the never-stopping,
And the senseless frightening
Fate of being legs.

Legs for the road,
The road for legs,
Resolutely nowhere
In both directions.

My legs at least
Were not in that rout,
On grass by the road-side
Entire I stood,

Watching the unstoppable
Legs go by
With never a stumble
Between step and step.

Though my smile was broad
The legs could not see,
Though my laugh was loud
The legs could not hear.

My head dizzied then :
I wondered suddenly,
Might I too be a walker
From the knees down ?

Gently I touched my shins.
The doubt unchained them :
They had run in twenty puddles
Before I regained them.

Robert Graves.

64. THE WRETCH

LIKE a lizard in the sun, though not scuttling
    When men approach, this wretch, this thing of
      rage,
Scowls and sits rhyming in his horny age.

His time and truth he has not bridged to ours,
But shrivelled by long heliotropic idling
He croaks at us his out of date humours.

Once long ago here was a poet ; who died.
See how remorse twitching his mouth proclaims
The case was murder, never suicide.

Arrogant, deaf, unvenerable, he
Still turns for comfort to the western flames
That glitter cold a span above the sea.

Robert Graves.

65. TO WALK ON HILLS

To walk on hills is to employ legs
   As porters of the head and heart
Jointly adventuring towards
Perhaps true equanimity.

To walk on hills is to see sights
And hear sounds unfamiliar.
When in wind the pine-tree roars,
When crags with bleatings echo,
When water foams below the fall,
Heart records that journey
As memorable indeed ;
Head reserves opinion,
Confused by the wind.

A view of three shires and the sea!
Seldom so much at once appears
Of the coloured world, says heart.
Head is glum, says nothing.
Legs become weary, halting
To sprawl in a rock's shelter,
While the sun drowsily blinks
On head at last brought low—
This giddied passenger of legs
That has no word to utter.

Heart does double duty,
As heart, and as head,
With portentous trifling.

A castle on its crag perched
Across the miles between is viewed
With awe as across years.
Now a daisy pleases,
Pleases and astounds, even,
That on a garden lawn could blow
All summer long with no esteem.
And the buzzard's horrid poise,
And the plover's misery,
And the important beetle's
Blue-green-shiny back . . .

To walk on hills is to employ legs
To march away and lose the day.
Confess, have you known shepherds ?
And are they not a witless race
Prone to quaint visions ?
Not thus from solitude
(Solitude sobers only)
But from long hilltop striding.

Robert Graves.

66. THE EXILE

INTO exile with only a few shirts,
    Some gold coin and the necessary papers.
But winds are contrary : the Channel packet
Time after time returns the sea-sick peer
To Sandwich, Deal or Rye.   He does not land,
But keeps his cabin ; so at last we find him
In humble lodgings at perhaps Dieppe,
His shirts unpacked, his night-cap on a peg,

Passing the day with cards and swordsmanship
Or merry passages with chambermaids,
By night at his old work.   And all is well—
The country wine wholesome although so sharp,
And French his second tongue ; a faithful valet
Brushes his hat and brings him newspapers.
This nobleman is at home anywhere,
His castle being, the valet says, his title.
The cares of an estate would incommode
Such tasks as now his Lordship has in hand.
His Lordship, says the valet, contemplates
A profitable absence of some years.
Has he no friend at Court to intercede ?
He wants none : exile's but another name
For an old habit of non-residence
In all but the recesses of his cloak.
It was this angered a great personage.

Robert Graves.

67. THE QUIDS

THE little quids, the monstrous quids,
    The everywhere, everything, always quids,
The atoms of the Monoton,
Each turned an essence where it stood,
Ground a gisty dust from its neighbours' edges,
Until a powdery thoughtfall stormed in and out—
The cerebration of a slippery quid enterprise.

Each quid stirred.
The united quids
Waved through a sinuous decision.

The quids, that had never done anything before
But be, be, be, be, be—
The quids resolved to predicate,
To dissipate themselves in grammar.

Oh, the Monoton didn't care,
For whatever they did—
The Monoton's contributing quids—
The Monoton would always remain the same.

A quid here and there gyrated in place-position,
While many turned inside-out for the fun of it.
And a few refused to be anything but
Simple unpredicated copulatives.
Little by little, this commotion of quids,
By ones, by tens, by casual millions,
Squirming within the state of things,
The metaphysical acrobats,
The naked, immaterial quids,
Turned in on themselves
And came out all dressed—
Each similar quid of the inward same,
Each similar quid dressed in a different way,
The quids' idea of a holiday.

The quids could never tell what was happening.
But the Monoton felt itself differently the same
In its different parts.
The silly quids upon their learned exercise
Never knew, could never tell
What their wisdom was about,

What their carnival was like,
Being in, being in, being always in
Where they never could get out
Of the everywhere, everything, always in,
To derive themselves from the Monoton.

Laura Riding.

68. AS MANY QUESTIONS AS ANSWERS

WHAT is to start ?
        It is to have feet to start with.
What is to end ?
It is to have nothing to start again with,
And not to wish.

What is to see ?
It is to know in part.
What is to speak ?
It is to add part to part
And make a whole
Of much or little.
What is to whisper ?
It is to make soft
The greed of speaking faster
Than is substance for.
What is to cry out ?
It is to make gigantic
Where speaking cannot last long.

What is to be ?
It is to bear a name.

What is to die ?
It is to be name only.
And what is to be born ?
It is to choose the enemy self
To learn impossibility from.
And what is to have hope ?
Is it to choose a god weaker than self,
And pray for compliments ?

What is to ask ?
It is to find an answer.
What is to answer ?
Is it to find a question ?

Laura Riding.

69. EARTH

Have no wide fears for Earth :
   Its universal name is " Nowhere."
If it is Earth to you, that is your secret.
The outer records leave off there,
And you may write it as it seems,
And as it seems, it is,
A seeming stillness
Amidst seeming speed.

Heavens unseen, or only seen,
Dark or bright space, unearthly space,
Is a time before Earth was
From which you inward move
Toward perfect now.

Almost the place it is not yet,
Potential here of everywhere—
Have no wide fears for it :
Its destiny is simple,
To be further what it will be.

Earth is your heart
Which has become your mind
But still beats ignorance
Of all it knows—
As miles deny the compact present
Whose self-mistrusting past they are.
Have no wide fears for Earth :
Destruction only on wide fears shall fall.

Laura Riding.

70. DOOM IN BLOOM

Now flower the oldest seeds.
　　The secret of the root no more
Keeps jealous distance from the air.
The dark intent, so loathfully ascending,
At last to resolution grows ;
The glance of long reluctance shows.

Weakly we write upon
The closing surface of oblivion.
Our faith in earth, in nether sameness,
Hurries to take the separate colour.
And leaning on the faded air
We flaunt ourselves against despair.

Gruesomely joined in hate
Of unlike efflorescence,
We were a cruel compacted silence
From which unlovable centuries sprang.
But time has knit so hard a crust
That speak and differ now we must—

Or be in pride encased
Until the living way has ceased
And only death comes to occur.
Though half our zeal but fair is,
Spells but an earth's variety,
Hope makes a stronger half to beauty

When from the deep bed torn
Of ultimate misgiving
An auspice of like peril to bring.
The lone defiance blossoms failure,
But risk of all by all beguiles
Fate's wreckage into similar smiles.

Laura Riding.

71. THE VICTORY

WITHOUT millions of pennies and millions of men
  Or nations of miles or five bolts of satin
Or six reams of fame to describe it upon
Or sixteen old castles to flag the news from
Or sixty new offices and their telephones—
Yet the business is done,
The great war is won,
The world has been made to know.

That it lies and denies
Or wears woe in disguise
Of its knowing, its joy so to know—
This is such pride as battalions of fire have
When a single cool drop quells the challenging blaze :
Of the drop not a sign, there's but reek of embers.
Thus smoulders the world, spitting hate of its baptism.
The last sparks tell not of healing, of cooling.

There is no news of knowledge in the newspapers.
Impregnable screens of vision have been raised
To protect the embattled minds from themselves.
A full peace has been visited now on the world,
But the voices of time do not mention it.
Nor think I to disturb
So much noise, nor to curb
So much fleeing from quiet's event.

Like a love that is loved
In a heart stiffly gloved
Against loveless responding event :
Though the face of the world with dim pain is con-
                          torted
As if the embrace were a forfended curse,
And the gift shall demand no more thanking than this,
Yet knowledge has been given, and knowledge taken.
Whether to weep or smile that truth conquers in
    secret ?

Laura Riding.

72. AFTER SO MUCH LOSS

AFTER so much loss—
        Seeming of gain,
Seeming of loss—
Subsides the swell of indignation
To the usual rhythm of the year.

The coward primroses are up,
We contract their profuse mildness.
Women with yet a few springs to live
Clutch them in supplicant bouquets
On the way to relatives,
Who, no, do not begrudge
This postponement of funerals.
And, oh, how never tired, and tired,
The world of primroses, how spring
The bended spirit fascinates
With promise of revival,
Leaving more honest summer to proclaim
That this is all—a brighter disappointment—
Time has to give to an implacable
Persuasion of things lost, wrongly.

Is it to wonder, then,
That we defy the unsuspecting moment,
Release our legs from the year's music,
And, to the reckless strum of hate,
Dance—grinding from primroses the tears
They never of themselves would have shed ?
None dances whom no hate stirs,
Who has not lost and loathed the loss,

Who does not feel deprived.
Slyest rebellion of the feet,
The chaste and tremulous disport
Of children, limbs in passionless wave—
None dances whom no hate stirs,
Or shall not stir.

As sure as primrosed spring betides,
After so much loss,
The hate will out, the dance be on,
And many of their rage fall down.
It is easy as spring to yield to the year,
And easy as dance to break with the year.
But to go with the year in partition
Between seeming loss, seeming gain,
That is the difficult decorum.
Nor are the primroses unwelcome.

Laura Riding.

73. III. WIR SIND ALLE VERLOREN

DARKNESS is in the hills, the eyes perish,
    The blinded spirit suffers and endures,
Knowing its degradation, whimpering, aching,
For comfort-earth, and sleep, and a child's simplicities.

Not for the hills, the flowers, the cheering people,
Not for a stubborn faith or world of knowledge,
Neither the substance nor the shadow,
These men died.

Ice brittle in the hair, the eyes blinded, inflamed,
Dragging reluctant bodies to the summit, forcing
Downward to humble earth, the cloud-born spirit,
They lived, enduring.

Angtsering, eight days in the blizzard :
" Up there the sahibs perished,   *Nanga*
That was where Wieland died, and there Herr Merkl. *Parbat*
It was cold, sahib, and we had no food."   1934

Others will die for a cause, the straining wind
Will tear the struggling root and scatter seed ;
These were the overflow, the bounty,
The useless petals falling—

Bennen, " the bravest guide the Valais ever had ", *Haut-de-*
Hearing the gathering hiss, the whole snowfield *Cry*
                                  slipping, 1864
Turning toward the valley and the gentians,
" Alle verloren ".

Bennen, lifting his arms at last toward the valley,
Or Carrel, caught in the tourmente and the lightning, *Matterhorn*
An old man, fighting, dying, the storm ended,   1890
Meine Herren safe.

Their eyes are ringed with flame, the cloud-born spirit
Burns in the living mind, returns to earth,
Distorting, twisting, breaking the living frame,
The petals falling.

There, in the darkened hills, the rain is falling,
The hills are ribbed with flame, the lightning falling,
The life, the venom, the storm-tormented hawk,
And the mind at rest.

Michael Roberts.

74. IN TIME OF PEACE

THERE is no quiet in the earth,
    In the green root of history, or the leaf
Bending toward the earth ;
In the brown eyes, the lake reflecting
Cumulus, cirrus, moving ;
Or in the water-sky, reflecting channels in the ice-pack;
In boundless, never-ending action, under, and in, and
over,
The sea reflecting,
There is no peace.

At Fleurier, in the shadow of the stone-pine,
At Langres, in the vineyard,
At Macugnaga,
There is no peace.

Bruno, in the Campo di Fiori, burning,
Hitler saluting,
Jules, remembering the orchard and the dead,
Marcel, rolling a cigarette, and Guillaume,
Scanning the frontier ridges for deserters or a chamois
These,

The building of a tower,
The meteor falling,
The shriek and shuddering of brakes,
The anguish in the windscreen, and the growth
Bursting, a secret flower ; the newsboy shouting :
These are normal.

There is no quiet in the turning sea,
Or under burning stone, or glacier ice ;
Under the guns, the summer corn, the Paramount,
Deeper than piercing worm or peering drill,
The blind earth cogitates, the lava moves :

There is no peace, there is no certainty,
There is no quiet but the solid earth : the times
—The stonefall and the clamouring and silence—
The times are normal.

Michael Roberts.

75. THE CASTLE

Words fall, words fail, like rocks, like falling stones;
    Out of the towered clouds and the dark air,
Words fail, and a tree of blackness falls :
There is nothing at all to surrender or defend.

It was a grim castle, built in the bad years,
Built by an old man after years of failure,
Stuccoed with long complacency, and now
No more than an empty wineskin or a crushed fruit.

From the dark earth, the tree broke out, and men
Died with a frantic zeal, and spitting death :

Who knows what it was they died for ?
Their bones are a fine dust, and their names forgotten.

Suburbs creep up the hill, and the trams are running,
Children find ghostly playmates in the ruins ;
The sun glares on the emptiness, and vanished walls
Burn with a bitter death and unfulfilled perfection.

Stamp out the memory of old wars and lost causes,
Build a grave citadel of peace, or a tower of death :
The castle stands, inhuman, incorruptible,
Like a film before the eyes, or a mad vision.

Michael Roberts.

76. LA MARCHE DES MACHINES
(Suggested by Deslav's film)

THIS piston's infinite recurrence is
    night morning night and morning night and
death and birth and death and birth and this
crank climbs (blind Sisyphus) and see

steel teeth greet
bow deliberate
delicately lace
in lethal kiss
    God's teeth bite whitely tight

slowly the gigantic oh slowly the steel spine dis-
    locates
wheels grazing (accurately missing) waltz
two cranes do a hundred-ton tango against the sky.

A. S. J. Tessimond.

77. LIVE YOU BY LOVE CONFINED . . .

LIVE you by love confined,
  There is no nearer nearness;
Break not his light bounds,
The stars' and seas' harness:
There is nothing beyond,
We have found the land's end.
We'll take no mortal wound
Who felt him in the furnace,
Drowned in his fierceness,
By his midsummer browned:
Nor ever lose awareness
Of nearness and farness
Who've stood at earth's heart careless
Of suns and storms around,
Who have leant on the hedge of the wind,
On the last ledge of darkness.

We are where love has come
To live: he is that river
Which flows and is the same;
He is not the famous deceiver
Nor early-flowering dream.
Content you. Be at home
In me. There's but one room
Of all the house you may never
Share, deny or enter.
There, as a candle's beam
Stands firm and will not waver
Spire straight in a close chamber,
As though in shadowy cave a

Stalagmite of flame,
The integral spirit climbs
The dark in light for ever.

Cecil Day Lewis.

78. A TIME TO DANCE

FOR those who had the power
    of the forest fires that burn
Leaving their source in ashes
    to flush the sky with fire :
Those whom a famous urn
    could not contain, whose passion
Brimmed over the deep grave
    and dazzled epitaphs :
For all that have won us wings
    to clear the tops of grief,
My friend who within me laughs
    bids you dance and sing.

Some set out to explore
    earth's limit, and little they recked if
Never their feet came near it
    outgrowing the need for glory :
Some aimed at a small objective
    but the fierce updraught of their spirit
Forced them to the stars.
        Are honoured in public who built
The dam that tamed a river ;
    or holding the salient for hours

Against odds, cut off and killed,
        are remembered by one survivor.

All these.   But most for those
        whom accident made great,
As a radiant chance encounter
        of cloud and sunlight grows
Immortal on the heart :
        whose gift was the sudden bounty
Of a passing moment, enriches
        the fulfilled eye for ever.
Their spirits float serene
        above time's roughest reaches,
But their seed is in us and over
        our lives they are evergreen.

                              Cecil Day Lewis.

79. MOONLIGHT, WATERLIGHT AND OPAL

"Moonlight, Waterlight and Opal are good
        Corinthians, bad friends for a young man,"
Said I, crone-like in my self-motherhood—
Jealous, perhaps, for the more homely clan.

I loved their glitter, like a mirror's face
Held to my revel with such flattering care.
And when it might have tarnished, with what grace
Moonlight, Waterlight, Opal were not there !

These moonbeam niceties, sweet to undergo,
Have been an austere discipline, the less

Exceptionable in that trifling so
I learned to be content with nothingness.
Norman Cameron.

80. THE FUTURE IS NOT FOR US

THE future is not for us, though we can set up
　　Our barriers, rest in our dead-embered
Sphere, till we come to pause over our last loving-cup
With death.　We are dismembered
Into a myriad broken shadows,
Each to himself reflected in a splinter of that glass
Which we once knew as cosmos, and the close
Of our long progress is hinted by the crass
Fogs creeping slow and darkly
From out the middle west.　We can humanize,
We can build new temples for the body,
Set our intellect to tilt against the spies
Of fortune, call this Chance or that Fate,
Estimate the logical worth of " it may depend . . . ,"
But we know that we are at the gate
Leading out of the path
Which was to be an Amen having neither beginning
　　nor end.

It was said, " Take no thought for the morrow ";
Better, truly, to take no thought of to-day,
For we are bankrupt indeed if we cannot borrow
At least an expectation of future pay.
Remains then but to seize
Each one alone, his smoky taper

And climb the stairs, knowing each step in the rear
Has crumpled beneath like tissue paper,
Disclosing the blue-black inkblot
Of vacuity beneath our sinking knees ;
Then to set our fingers on the latch with the hope or
    fear
That within there lies the Is or Is Not.

Ronald Bottrall.

81. ARION ANADYOMENOS
(Storm on a Sunday Evening)

WE are sitting in a swimming air
    Swept by the rain phalanx, talking drily
Of Noah in the flood season. " Repair
The beams and rafters, let the light lie
Heavy on our roofs provided we may rest unhaunted
By threats of entombment
Being yet unhouseled, unwanted."

Within, the toothless beldam purrs applause
At the nice posture of our slippered feet
Uneager to exert her adept jaws
On the stringy unsubstantial meat
Or her brain on the mould of a remainder biscuit.
Outside a black row of sycamores
Re-rank their tops from out the mist
Saddled, however, by no Zaccheus
To invite attention from the Paraclete,
A dove content, assuredly, with his olive branch
And sworn foe to the syllogist.

" We are three of us here and the passing
Of day, the sight of a spider
Walking the wall, or the patter of ashes
As they drop on the hearth have,
For our palates, a varied piquancy,
Objects angled from three compass points
And thus irreconcilable.   Nor do these alone
Move through contraries, for often
Our delights are childed on our fears
And we sin from an excess
Of righteousness."

Implications of our pedigree
Cleave this whirl of light and shade,
No room to allot the praise here or agree
Upon an exegesis of the crime.   The horoscope
Our fathers cast has set our teeth on edge ;
See, they have shortened this man's scope,
Crippled him for private ends
And sent him down the wind, a pledge
To be redeemed in the Greek Kalends.

" Is it worth while to make lips smile again,
To transmit that uneasiness in us which craves
A moment's mouthing, craves to bully the pain
The pain and pity of it into staves
Of crabbed pothooks, filling the breadth
Of title-page to colophon ?
Is it worth while to debate upon
The automatic sense which forces us
To circumvent our quietus

And put instead on record
Reactions to the vibrations of a vocal cord ? ”

The waters are lifting at length, and stand revealed
The shoddy roofs steeled,
Even silvered, by reflected light, quite rent
From their cadaverous cerement,
While the final passacaglia of Brahms
Weaves itself point by point
Into the shuddering waves of rain,
Assertive, affirmative, triumphant . . .
Perchance, after all, living within
And for ourselves, exhaling our entity
In our perceptions, yet not altogether bent
With our breaths to petrify and eternize
Some stony replica, we have tracked
What song the sirens sang.   So may the disjoint
Time resolve itself and raise up dolphins backed
Like whales to waft us where a confident sea
Is ever breaking, never spent.

Ronald Bottrall.

82. PREAMBLE TO A GREAT ADVENTURE

WE’LL cut the cackle about attainment
    And overhaul the chassis and accessories.
You are accustomed to wear a reticulated
Monocle and see the earth in
Strategical areas , acquire
A habit of thinking of men as a
Fluctuating pattern in fours.   Your

Ears have been established from birth
As delicately graduated filters, and your range
Of wave-lengths severely limited, but do not
Forget the efficacy of cotton wool.
I should advise you to instal
A panatrope in your lungs furnished
With tungstyle needles and twenty
Long-playing records guaranteed by
A professorial committee to perpetuate
The national gentlemanly sporting spirit
Of test matches and military tattoos.

Make no mistake about colour.
Offered an array of bonbons at a fashionable
Tea-party select the pink carmine-filled,
Toy with the white and show a marked
Distaste for gamboge and chocolate.
(Tactful hostesses indeed omit the last.)
Tricoloured hard centres are perhaps
To be preferred above all.
It is a precautionary measure
With many employers to submit applicants
To an automatic phonetic tester which
Deletes those not favoured with a cleft palate.
But this for you is an easy hurdle.

Turn yourself daily on the new lathe
Distributed gratis with every penny newspaper
Through the personal beneficence of
Directors of the leading armament firms ;

Strive to shape the grooves as spirals
Flowering into the upper air—
An image antique, beautiful and Greek;
The chemist will supply you with a ballast
Of explosive pellets for your nerves.
If your mind generates timid leprosies,
Slimy nightmares, or any other form
Of thought, give it a scouring with
Some healthy narrative of life
In the Foreign Legion.
Endless probings along corridors, sudden
Drops towards cesspools, the embrace
Of giant squids are common derangements:
Cure them with the Book of the Month.

Make ready the firm unseeing mind
And the strict co-ordination of muscle, pack
The hypodermic syringe.
Hold yourself taut
For the supreme moment of amputation,
Given you once and once only.
There is no dialectic but death's,
And the spider weaves over to-morrow.
There is no grasping of Valhalla,
No mitigation of purgatory,
No merging into Nirvana,
But allegiance to the wind that is sown
And joyful faith in the whirlwind that shall be reaped.
Man maimed and bleeding is a symbol
Firing us against detraction, yet of all
We do not exact heroics.   For the high

There are glittering prizes,
And the low have some honour.   Sacrifice,
The quiet submission to bacilli,
To throttling, lung-rotting gases, to the great
Will of the people, we readily accept.

Ronald Bottrall.

83. THE WITNESSES

I

You dowagers with Roman noses
  Sailing along between banks of roses
                          well dressed,
You Lords who sit at committee tables
And crack with grooms in riding stables
                          your father's jest;

Solicitors with poker faces,
And doctors with black bags to cases
                          hurried,
Reporters coming home at dawn
And heavy bishops on the lawn
                          by sermons worried;

You stokers lit by furnace-glare,
And you, too, steeplejacks up there
                          singing,
You shepherds wind-blown on the ridges,
Tramps leaning over village bridges
                          your eardrums ringing;

On land, on sea, in field, in town
Attend ; Musician put them down,
> those trumpets ;
Let go, young lover, of her hand
Come forward both of you and stand
> as still as limpets

Close as you can and listen well
My companion here is about to tell
> a story ;
Peter, Pontius Pilate, Paul
Whoever you are, it concerns you all
> and human glory.

II

Call him Prince Alpha if you wish
He was born in a palace, his people were swish ;
> his christening
Was called by the Tatler the event of the year,
All the photographed living were there
> and the dead were listening.

You would think I was trying to foozle you
If I told you all that kid could do ;
> enough
To say he was never afraid of the dark
He climbed all the trees in his pater's park ;
> his nurse thought him rough.

At school his brilliance was a mystery,
All languages, science, maths, and history
                                    he knew ;
His style at cricket was simply stunning
At rugger, soccer, hockey, running
                                     and swimming too.

The days went by, he grew mature ;
He was a looker you may be sure,
                                     so straight
Old couples cried, " God bless my soul
I thought that man was a telegraph pole "
                                     when he passed their gate.

His eyes were blue as a mountain lake,
He made the hearts of the girls to ache ;
                                     he was strong ;
He was gay, he was witty, his speaking voice
Sounded as if a large Rolls-Royce
                                     had passed along.

He kissed his dear old mater one day,
He said to her " I'm going away,
                                     good bye "
No sword nor terrier by his side
He set off through the world so wide
                                     under the sky.

Where did he travel ? Where didn't he travel
Over the ice and over the gravel
                                     and the sea ;

Up the fevered jungle river,
Through haunted forests without a shiver
                        he wandered free.

What did he do ? What didn't he do,
He rescued maidens, overthrew
                        ten giants
Like factory chimneys, slaughtered dragons,
Though their heads were larger than railway waggons
                        tamed their defiance.

What happened, what happened ? I'm coming to
    that ;
He came to a desert and down he sat
                        and cried
Above the blue sky arching wide
Two tall rocks as black as pride
                        on either side.

There on a stone he sat him down,
Around the desert stretching brown
                        like the tide,
Above the blue sky arching wide
Two black rocks on either side
                        and, O how he cried.

" I thought my strength could know no stemming
But I was foolish as a lemming ;
                        for what
Was I born, was it only to see
I'm as tired of life as life of me ?
                        let me be forgot.

Children have heard of my every action
It gives me no sort of satisfaction
                            and why ?
Let me get this as clear as I possibly can
No, I am not the truly strong man,
                            O let me die."

There in the desert all alone
He sat for hours on a long flat stone
                            and sighed ;
Above the blue sky arching wide
Two black rocks on either side,
                            and then he died.

Now ladies and gentlemen, big and small,
This story of course has a morale ;
                            again
Unless like him you wish to die
Listen, while my friend and I
                            proceed to explain.

III

What had he done to be treated thus ?
If you want to know, he'd offended us :
                            for yes,
We guard the wells, we're handy with a gun,
We've a very special sense of fun,
                            we curse and bless.

You are the town, and we are the clock,
We are the guardians of the gate in the rock,
                         the Two ;
On your left, and on your right
In the day, and in the night
                         we are watching you.

Wiser not to ask just what has occurred
To them that disobeyed our word ;
                         to those
We were the whirlpool, we were the reef,
We were the formal nightmare, grief,
                         and the unlucky rose.

Climb up the cranes, learn the sailors' words
When the ships from the islands, laden with birds
                         come in ;
Tell you stories of fishing, and other men's wives,
The expansive moments of constricted lives,
                         in the lighted inn.

By all means say of the peasant youth
" That person there is in the truth "
                         we're kind
Tire of your little rut and look it,
You have to obey but you don't have to like it,
                         we do not mind :

But do not imagine we do not know
Or that what you hide with care won't show
                         at a glance ;

Nothing is done, nothing is said
But don't make the mistake of thinking us dead ;
         I shouldn't dance

For I'm afraid in that case you'll have a fall ;
We've been watching you over the garden wall
         for hours,
The sky is darkening like a stain,
Something is going to fall like rain
         and it won't be flowers.

When the green field comes off like a lid
Revealing what were much better hid,
         unpleasant ;
And look ! behind without a sound
The woods have come up and are standing round
         in deadly crescent.

And the bolt is sliding in its groove,
Outside the window is the black remov-
         ers van,
And now with sudden swift emergence
Come the women in dark glasses, the hump-backed
         surgeons
         and the scissor-man.

This might happen any day
So be careful what you say
         or do
Be clean, be tidy, oil the lock
Trim the garden, wind the clock
         Remember the Two.
         W. H. Auden.

84. LOOK, STRANGER, . . .

Look, stranger, at this island now
    The leaping light for your delight discovers,
Stand stable here
And silent be,
That through the channels of the ear
May wander like a river
The swaying sound of the sea.

Here at the small field's ending pause
Where the chalk wall falls to the foam, and its tall ledges
Oppose the pluck
And knock of the tide,
And the shingle scrambles after the suck-
ing surf, and the gull lodges
A moment on its sheer side.

Far off like floating seeds the ships
Diverge on urgent voluntary errands ;
And the full view
Indeed may enter
And move in memory as now these clouds do,
That pass the harbour mirror
And all the summer through the water saunter.

W. H. Auden.

85. LETTER TO LORD BYRON
Part V

Autumn is here.   The beech leaves strew the lawn ;
    The power stations take up heavier loads ;
The massive lorries shake from dusk till dawn

The houses on the residential roads ;
The shops are full of coming winter modes.
Dances have started at the Baths next door
Stray scraps of MS strew my bedroom floor.

I read that there's a boomlet on in Birmingham,
    But what I hear is not so reassuring ;
Rumours of War, the B.B.C. confirming 'em,
    The prospects for the future aren't alluring ;
    No one believes Prosperity enduring,
Not even Wykehamists, whose golden mean
Maintains the All Souls' Parish Magazine.

The crack between employees and employers
    Is obvious already as the nose on
John Gielgud's face ; the keels of new destroyers
    Get laid down somehow though all credit's frozen ;
    The Pope's turned protestant at last and chosen,
Thinking it safer in the temporal circs,
The Italian faith against the Russian works.

England, my England—you have been my tutrix—
    The Mater, on occasions, of the free,
Or, if you'd rather, Dura Virum Nutrix,
    Whatever happens I am born of Thee ;
    And Englishmen, all foreigners agree,
Taking them by and large, and as a nation,
All suffer from an Oedipus fixation.

With all thy faults, of course we love thee still ;
    We'd better for we have to live with you,

From Rhondda Valley or from Bredon Hill,
    From Rotherhithe, or Regent Street, or Kew
    We look you up and down and whistle 'Phew !
Mother looks odd to-day dressed up in peers,
Slums, aspidistras, shooting-sticks, and queers'.

Cheer up ! There're several singing birds that sing.
    There's six feet six of Spender for a start ;
Eliot has really stretched his eagle's wing,
    And Yeats has helped himself to Parnell's heart ;
    This book has samples of MacNeice's art ;
There's Wyndham Lewis fuming out of sight,
That lonely old volcano of the Right.

I'm marking time because I cannot guess
    The proper place to which to send this letter,
c/o Saint Peter or The Infernal Press ?
    I'll try the Press.   World-culture is its debtor ;
    It has a list that Faber's couldn't better.
For Heaven gets all the lookers for her pains,
But Hell, I think, gets nearly all the brains.

The congregation up there in the former
    Are those whose early upbringing was right,
Who never suffered from a childish trauma ;
    As babies they were Truby King's delight ;
    They're happy, lovely, but not overbright.
For no one thinks unless a complex makes him
Or till financial ruin overtakes him.

Complex or Poverty ; in short The Trap.
  Some set to work to understand the spring ;
Others sham dead, pretend to take a nap ;
  " It is a motor-boat," the madmen sing ;
  The artist's action is the queerest thing :
He seems to like it, couldn't do without it,
And only wants to tell us all about it.

While Rome is burning or he's out of sorts
  " Causons, causons, mon bon," he's apt to say,
" What does it matter while I have these thoughts ? "
  Or so I've heard, but Freud's not quite O.K.
  No artist works a twenty-four hour day.
In bed, asleep or dead, it's hard to tell
The highbrow from l'homme moyen sensuel.

" Es neiget die weisen zu schönem sich."
  Your lordship's brow that never wore a hat
Should thank your lordship's foot that did the trick.
  Your mother in a temper cried, " Lame Brat ! "
  Posterity should thank her much for that.
Had she been sweet she surely would have taken
Juan away and saved your moral bacon.

The match of Hell and Heaven was a nice
  Idea of Blake's, but won't take place, alas.
You can choose either, but you can't choose twice ;
  You can't, at least in this world, change your class ;
  Neither is alpha plus though both will pass :
And don't imagine you can write like Dante,
Dive like your nephew, crochet like your auntie.

The Great Utopia, free of all complexes,
    The Withered State is, at the moment, such
A dream as that of being both the sexes,
    I like Wolf's *Goethe-lieder* very much,
    But doubt if *Ganymede's* appeal will touch—
That marvellous cry with its ascending phrases—
Capitalism in its later phases.

Are Poets saved ? Well, let's suppose they are,
    And take a peep.   I don't see any books.
Shakespeare is lounging grandly at the bar,
    Milton is dozing, judging by his looks,
    Shelley is playing poker with two crooks,
Blake's adding pince-nez to an ad. for players,
Chaucer is buried in the latest Sayers.

Lord Alfred rags with Arthur on the floor,
    Housman, all scholarship forgot at last,
Sips up the stolen waters through a straw,
    Browning's complaining that Keats bowls too fast,
    And you have been composing as they passed
A clerihew on Wordsworth and his tie,
A rather dirty limerick on Pye.

I hope this reaches you in your abode,
    This letter that's already far too long,
Just like the Prelude or the Great North Road ;
    But here I end my conversational song.
    I hope you don't think mail from strangers wrong.
As to its length, I tell myself you'll need it,
You've all eternity in which to read it.

                              W. H. Auden.

86. LEGAL FICTION

Law makes long spokes of the short stakes of men.
  Your well fenced out real estate of mind
No high flat of the nomad citizen.
Looks over, or train leaves behind.

Your rights extend under and above your claim
Without bound ; you own land in Heaven and Hell ;
Your part of earth's surface and mass the same,
Of all cosmos' volume, and all stars as well.

Your rights reach down where all owners meet, in Hell's
Pointed exclusive conclave, at earth's centre
(Your spun farm's root still on that axis dwells) ;
And up, through galaxies, a growing sector.

You are nomad yet ; the lighthouse beam you own
Flashes, like Lucifer, through the firmament.
Earth's axis varies ; your dark central cone
Wavers, a candle's shadow, at the end.

William Empson.

87. SONG

The sunlight on the garden
  Hardens and grows cold,
We cannot cage the minute
Within its nets of gold ;
When all is told
We cannot beg for pardon.

Our freedom as free lances
Advances towards its end ;
The earth compels, upon it
Sonnets and birds descend ;
And soon, my friend,
We shall have no time for dances.

The sky was good for flying
Defying the church bells
And every evil iron
Siren and what it tells :
The earth compels,
We are dying, Egypt, dying

And not expecting pardon,
Hardened in heart anew,
But glad to have sat under
Thunder and rain with you,
And grateful too
For sunlight on the garden.

Louis MacNeice.

88. THE CREDITOR

THE quietude of a soft wind
    Will not rescind
My debts to God, but gentle-skinned
His finger probes.   I lull myself
In quiet in diet in riot in dreams,
In dopes in drams in drums in dreams
Till God retire and the door shut.

But
Now I am left in the fire-blaze
The peacefulness of the fire-blaze
Will not erase
My debts to God for His mind strays
Over and under and all ways
All days and always.

Louis MacNeice.

89. ECLOGUE BY A FIVE-BARRED GATE
(Death and Two Shepherds)

D. There is no way here, shepherds, read the wooden
   sign,
   Your road is a blind road, all this land is mine.
1. But your fields, mister, would do well for our sheep.
2. They could shelter from the sun where the low hills
   dip.
D. I have sheep of my own, see them over there.
1. There seems no nater in 'em, they look half dead.
2. They be no South Downs, they look so thin and bare.
D. More than half, shepherds, they are more than half
   dead.
   But where are your own flocks you have been so talk-
   ing of ?
1. Right here at our elbow—
2.   Or they *was* so just now.
D. That's right, shepherd, they was so just now.
   Your sheep are gone, they can't speak for you,
   I must have your credentials, sing me who you are.
1. I am a shepherd of the Theocritean breed.

Been pasturing my songs, man and boy, this thirty
    year—
2. And for me too my pedigree acceptances
Have multiplied beside the approved streams.
D. This won't do, shepherds, life is not like that,
And when it comes to death I may say he is not like
    that.
Have you never thought of Death?
1.   Only off and on,
Thanatos in Greek, the accent proparoxytone—
2. That's not what he means, he means the thing behind
    the word
Same as took Alice White the time her had her third—
D. Cut out for once the dialect and the pedantry,
I thought a shepherd was a poet—
1.   On his flute—
2.   On his oat—
D. I thought he was a poet and could quote the prices
Of significant living and decent dying, could lay the
    rails level on the sleepers
To carry the powerful train of abstruse thought—
1. What an idea!
2.   But certainly poets are sleepers,
The sleeping beauty behind the many-coloured
    hedge—
D. All you do is burke the other and terrible beauty, all
    you do is hedge
And shirk the inevitable issue, all you do
Is shear your sheep to stop your ears.
Poetry you think is only the surface vanity,
The painted nails, the hips narrowed by fashion,

The hooks and eyes of words ; but it is not that only,
And it is not only the curer sitting by the wayside,
Phials on his trestle, his palms grown thin as wafers
With blessing the anonymous heads ;
And poetry is not only the bridging of two-banked
     rivers.

2. Whoever heard of a river without a further bank ?

D. You two never heard of it.
Tell me now, I have heard the cuckoo, there is tar on
     your shoes,
I surmise that spring is here—

2.   Spring be here truly,
On Bank Holiday I wore canvas shoes,
Could feel the earth—

D.   And that being so, tell me
Don't you ever feel old ?

2.   There's a question now.

1. It is a question we all have to answer,
And I may say that when I smell the beans or hear the
     thrush
I feel a wave intensely bitter-sweet and topped with
     silver—

D. There you go again, your self-congratulation
Blunts all edges, insulates with wool
No spark of reality possible.
Can't you peel off for even a moment that conscious
     face.
All time is not your tear-off jotter, you cannot afford
     to scribble
So many so false answers.
This escapism of yours is blasphemy,

An immortal cannot blaspheme for one way or
    another
His trivialities will pattern in the end ;
But for you your privilege and panic is to be mortal
And with Here and Now for your anvil
You must strike while the iron is hot—
2.   He is an old man,
That is why he talks so.
D.   Can't you understand me ?
Look, I will set you a prize like any of your favourites,
Like any Tityrus or tired Damon ;
Sing me, each in turn, what dream you had last
    night
And if either's dream rings true, to him I will open
    my gate :
2. Ho, here's talking.
1.   Let me collect myself.
D. Collect yourself in time for if you win my prize—
2. I'm going to sing first, I had a rare dream.
1. Your dream is nothing—
D.   The more nothing the better.
1. My dream will word well—
2.   But not wear well—
D. No dreams wear at all as dreams.
Water appears tower only while in well—
All from the same comes, the same drums sound
In the pulsation of all the bulging suns,
And no clock whatever, while winding or running
    down,
Makes any difference to time however the long-legged
    weights

Straggle down the cottage wall or the child grows
  leggy too—
1. I do not like your talking.
2.   It gives giddiness
Like the thrumming of the telephones wires in an
  east wind
With the bellyache and headache and nausea.
D. It is not my nature to talk, so sing your pieces
And I will try, what is repugnant too, to listen.
1. Last night as the bearded lips of sleep
Closed with the slightest sigh on me and I sank
  through the blue soft caves
Picked with light delicate as the chink of coins
Or stream on the pebbles I was caught by hands
And a face was swung in my eyes like a lantern
Swinging on the neck of a snake.
And that face I knew to be God and I woke,
And now I come to look at yours, stranger,
There is something in the lines of it—
D.   Your dream, shepherd,
Is good enough of its kind. Now let us hear yours.
2. Well, I dreamt it was a hot day, the territorials
Were out on melting asphalt under the howitzers,
The brass music bounced on the houses. Come
I heard cry as it were a water-nymph, come and ful-
  fil me
And I sped floating, my feet plashing in the tops of
  the wheat
But my eyes were blind,
I found her with my hands lying on the drying hay,
Wet heat in the deeps of the hay as my hand delved,

And I possessed her, gross and good like the hay,
And she went and my eyes regained sight and the sky
    was full of ladders
Angels ascending and descending with a shine like
    mackerel—
Now I come to tell it it sounds nonsense.
D. Thank you, gentlemen, these two dreams are good,
Better than your daytime madrigals.
If you really wish I will give you both the prize,
But take another look at my land before you choose
    it.
1. It looks colder now.
2.   The sheep have not moved.
1. I have a fancy there is no loving there
Even among sheep.
D.   They do not breed or couple
1 & 2. And what about us, shall we enjoy it there?
D. *Enjoy what where?*
2.   Why, life in your land.
D. I will open this gate that you may see for yourselves.
1. You go first.
2.   Well, you come too.
1 & 2. We will go together to these pastures new . . .
D. So; they are gone; life in my land . . .
There is no life as there is no land.
They are gone and I am alone.
With a gate the façade of a mirage.

Louis MacNeice.

90. THIS EXCELLENT MACHINE

This excellent machine is neatly planned,
    A child, a half-wit would not feel perplexed :
No chance to err, you simply press the button—
At once each cog in motion moves the next,
The whole revolves, and anything that lives
Is quickly sucked towards the running band,
Where, shot between the automatic knives,
It's guaranteed to finish dead as mutton.

This excellent machine will illustrate
The Modern World divided into nations :
So neatly planned, that if you merely tap it
The armaments will start their devastations,
And though we're for it, though we're all convinced
Some fool will press the button soon or late,
We stand and stare, expecting to be minced,—
And very few are asking, *Why not scrap it ?*

John Lehmann.

91. A LITTLE DISTANCE OFF

This world behind the faces that you see,
    The moving lips and eyelids, eyes alight
Like matches blown by wind, because you stand
A little distance off and cannot change
Your isolation for their many, bears
The complete shape of art, the harmony
And pattern of a film. . . . The film unrolls,
The world evolves in words and flame of eyes,
And you withdrawn, a watcher, yet create,
Yet mould the shape, alter a pose or smile,

The incidence of light, as one who sees
Across the windows of a climbing train
The mountain farms curl backwards, where the paths
Lead up to glimpses of sun dazzled walls,
Conceives strange lives and features, faintly hearing
The fall of music from behind the trees.

John Lehmann.

92. FATA MORGANA

LAST night as I was marching on the road
That leads my unknown comrades to the wars
I was more free and happy as I trod
White dust between the dark and shadeless trees.

There was a village with no people left
It was like England, but it was in Spain,
The awnings were in ribbons on their posts,
We paused to look, and then marched on again.

The villagers had learned to know defeat,
We were not sure that vengeance could prevail.
The enemy was safe in his retreat,
And our advance was pretty sure to fail.

Did I then hope to reason with the guns ?
Or did I hope to pass the bullets by ?
And did I pity the old men whose sons
Upon the white plains are about to die ?

No, I had fear enough to keep me silent
And hope that soon the face of things might change.
It was an ordinary and dull event
To shorten mile by mile the rifle's range.

I am no longer, alas, a charmed life,
One whom the gods will favour, ill can spare,
But target for the bullet and the knife
Like any other soldier, wolf, or hare.

Yet it was brave to keep our secrets close
That we had once had egoism to lose.
We swallowed back our pride, obeying orders
From leaders that in wiser days we chose.

It is remarkable to dream so much
And yet wake up to spend another day
With all the people we can only touch
With tales of long ago and far away.

                                        K. J. Raine.

93. I THINK CONTINUALLY . . .

I THINK continually of those who were truly great.
    Who, from the womb, remembered the soul's
        history
Through corridors of light where the hours are suns
Endless and singing. Whose lovely ambition
Was that their lips, still touched with fire,
Should tell of the Spirit clothed from head to foot in
        song.
And who hoarded from the Spring branches
The desires falling across their bodies like blossoms.

What is precious is never to forget
The essential delight of the blood drawn from ageless
        springs

Breaking through rocks in worlds before our earth.
Never to deny its pleasure in the morning simple light
Nor its grave evening demand for love.
Never to allow gradually the traffic to smother
With noise and fog the flowering of the spirit.

Near the snow, near the sun, in the highest fields
See how these names are fêted by the waving grass
And by the streamers of white cloud
And whispers of wind in the listening sky.
The names of those who in their lives fought for life
Who wore at their hearts the fire's centre.
Born of the sun they travelled a short while towards
    the sun,
And left the vivid air signed with their honour.

Stephen Spender.

94. IN 1929

A WHIM of Time, the general arbiter,
    Proclaims the love instead of death of friends.
Under the domed sky and athletic sun
The three stand naked : the new, bronzed German,
The communist clerk, and myself, being English.

Yet to unwind the travelled sphere twelve years
Then two take arms, spring to a ghostly posture.
Or else roll on the thing a further ten
And this poor clerk with world-offended eyes
Builds with red hands his heaven ; makes our bones
The necessary scaffolding to peace.

*   *   *   *

Now I suppose that the once-envious dead
Have learnt a strict philosophy of clay
After these centuries, to haunt us no longer
In the churchyard or at the end of the lane
Or howling at the edge of the city
Beyond the last beanrows, near the new factory.

Our fathers killed.   And yet there lives no feud
Like prompting Hamlet on the castle stair ;
There falls no shade across our blank of peace,
We being together, struck across our path,
Or taper finger threatening solitude.

Our fathers' misery, the dead man's mercy,
The cynic's mystery, weave a philosophy
That the history of man traced purely from dust
Was lipping skulls on the revolving rim
Or the posture of genius with the granite head bowed :

Lives risen a moment, joined or separate,
Fall heavily, then are always separate,
A stratum unreckoned by geologists,
Sod lifted, turned, slapped back again with spade.

Stephen Spender

95. CLIMBING A MOUNTAIN

"ADDÍO ! " " Addío ! " The guide and the guide's
wife
Tenderly, in the warm hut before dawn,
Parted after the breakfast by lamplight ;

And I went on, down the little path over the stream ;
The guide came with the rope and the other things
And led the way up silently between the fir-trees.

Up and up, on dogged metal my feet carried me,
Toward the distant shoulder ; above it hung
The watery and foreboding moon, fading.
In my eye was the grey light
And the guide pointing to signs of the War,
Brutal, jagged wire and tumble-down dugouts :
In my heart—but I did not know where my heart was,
Or why the rocks above me seemed more brutal,
Or my feet glad, carrying me up, out of the valley.

Dawn was above us, creeping down the white summit,
But we still were in twilight. I heard,
Under the scrunch of my feet across the gravel,
The stream's quick broken tumbling in the valley.
At last we reached the snow, and stopped. It was
                                        very lonely.
The guide undid his rucksack, saying something gay,
And we rigged ourselves out for crossing the snowfield.

I felt good in my legs, all dressed up like a Russian ;
But my heart hadn't come with me—I knew that now,
Panting and stumbling. I had no competence,
I felt feeble and small after a while
As I struggled up behind the mountaineer.

We had to keep stopping. I was so weary.
A little wind would blow over the desolate snowfield

And the guide would breathe it ; it was his breath.
When we came to rock again, it was the same :
He would look between rocks, down, down
Into the stony heart of the mountain,
And that would be his heart and the mountain-sides
                                             his sides.

When the wind dropped on the snowfield I would hear
The little stream bumping away in the valley,
And that would be my heart, I thought.
" Must you drone there always," I said, " will-less and
                                             idle ?
Come up and help me, skulker in the depth !
My legs are faint now, my blood is without ambition."
And my heart mumbled and became inaudible.

" Very well," I thought, " I will go on without you."
And on we went ; we kicked our way out of the snow
And began to ascend over the rock. By this time
The dawn had been swallowed up in a moist haze.
Soon I was quite without pride, and the climber's
                                             emulation ;
I let the guide haul me up over the difficult bits ;
I didn't care what he thought of me,
I didn't want to get to the top—
Except that it was probably the quickest way down
                                             now !

I was glad when I stumbled off the rock
And stood on the edge of the stone plateau.
The guide looked at the snow and back at the rock
And he loved them both with his eyes,

Like a child caressing its own innocent flesh.
Then, as we went on across the last level,
There seemed nothing to breathe ; I was unconscious ;
And there was nothing to see either, except the snow
Sodden with mist, and yielding ; leprous it seemed.

At the summit there was a book in a metal box.
We sat down and wrote in it solemnly.
I didn't look at the guide, I looked round me into the
                                                   mist.
We took out our food.   He gave me some red wine
                                           from his flask.
As he did so the flask clinked on the cup,
Hollow and dead in the rare, muffled quiet.
At last he spoke, slowly, in his soft clinging tongue—
A sort of congratulation, and something sad about the
                                                weather.

Well, this was the top.   In a way I was proud,
Though I'd nothing to be proud of, a failure in achieve-
                                                    ment.
I had lost my self, my heart, where the guide had
                                              found his.
My heart was down there all the time,
Perhaps now in the Albergo, singing songs and drink-
                                                     ing,
And laughing at the Italian tourists
(The little heads and the big chests)
Who buccaneered through their stolen country in
                                             shiny cars,
And the German tourists who came to gather plants.

But wasn't it good, my heart, to leave you for a while ?
Wasn't it good, for a few hours, to wrench myself
Out of the sun's embrace, the indolent valley,
To spurn you, to be alone, to be comfortless ?
Yes, churlish heart, it was good : to be lost
These long stolen hours from you—
First and most fulsome of counsellors.

James Reeves.

96. VISITORS TO THE WATERFALL

THEY see the rowan-trees above the fall,
    The broken rainbow at its base.
Moistened by spray, they scale the mountain wall;
    Their footsteps do not stumble
    Because almost a grace
    Is given by such elation
As violence with grandeur causes them,
    When, stunned past exclamation,
They hear the foam hiss and the waters tumble.

They will be safely down before the dark,
    And home before the summer ends.
The scarlet berries and the coloured arc
    The cataclysm and thunder
    They will describe to friends
    And photographs renew.
Then which of them would be surprised to feel
    His cheek grow cold with dew,
His pulse quicken, his breath stop short for wonder ?

They will not see the fragile rainbow fade
    The instant that the sun goes down.
Not dark nor autumn will their scene invade ;
        They will not see the red
        Transform to shrivelled brown,
        The rowan-berries fall
Of no account into unfertile crannies.
        But they will picture all
As it is, momentary, and nothing dead.

After the summer drought they will not hear
    The streams fail and the roar subside.
Then through the dwindling waters, hard and clear,
        The naked rock will show,
        Which now the waters hide.
        Such the true nature is
Of this bright mountain-country—at its heart
    A sunless gorge.   But this
For their vision's sake must visitors not know.

                              James Reeves.

97. SHAKESPEARE AND LATER

SHAKESPEARE was king of seasons,
    And ranged abundantly
The plain and pasture where they throve ;
Of climates,
The coloured levels of the sea and air.
From such visitations they grew noble,
Nor less magnificent
Than that wide-naming.

Then died such kingship,
Its provinces all dull, conquered.
Then came a mixing of the weathers
To make the vague pattern at the window.
Or the four winds blew at once,
Or all the four winds were hushed.
And we stood stubborn in the piight,
No name of wind or weather spoke—
Forbearing to rule, or claim
Pity as nature's exiles.
The empire of the elements was profuse
But seemlier from this late vantage
To leave the younger marvels nameless,
Scatter no more the gold of language.

Harry Kemp.

98. BLOCKING THE PASS

WITH an effort Grant swung the great block,
    The swivel operated and five or six men
Crouched under the lee of the straight rock.

They waited in silence or counting ten,
They thrust their fingers in their wet hair,
The steel sweated in their hands.   And then

The clouds hurried across a sky quite bare,
The sounds of the station, three miles off, ceased,
The dusty birds hopped keeping watch.   And there

Arose to what seemed as high as the sky at least,
Arose a giant and began to die,
Arose such a shape as the night in the East.

The stones sobbed, the trees gave a cry,
A tremulous wonder shook animal and plant,
And a decapitating anger stirred the sky

And alone, on a tall stone, stood Grant.

Charles Madge.

99. THE LOVES OF THE LIONS

UPON the borders of the desert is a town
     And the dust columns slowly pass that way
Concealing caravans and military stores
Which have come across the salty wasted sand
Between the sunny villages of the Moors.
It is a sad and dusty place by day
And small as a rock-spider in a hand
Whose jointed fingers might curve suddenly down.

But at night, when the last tram has gone home
And only one still searchlight searches the sky,
The cooling desert is alert with life
And mouths draw in breath which were shut all day
And mouths carnivorous for desert strife
Slow open the large caverns wherein creatures die ;
In reeds and bushes run the scurrying prey
And the stars chase along the desert hippodrome.

Where the smooth eyes of a woman all of stone
Unplanted with lashes, into sudden life
Melt quick as ice on meteors often found
Where the long stabbing cactus roots

Find moisture in the parched and gritty ground
Where humans lie asleep, large breathing fruits
Where sleeps the bearded chief and his smooth wife
Where shadows of the mountain sleep or groan.

Here run small coneys on their grassy tracks,
Pursuit of love that hurries here and there
And every insect people ; the moon in time
Floats, dangerous for an invading tribe.
And, as she curves the night, to hilltops climb
The lions and the lionesses, and inscribe
The night with journeys of each faithful pair.
An aeroplane sinks down above the iron stacks.

Charles Madge.

100. THE HAND THAT SIGNED THE PAPER...

THE hand that signed the paper felled a city ;
   Five sovereign fingers taxed the breath,
Doubled the globe of dead and halved a country ;
These five kings did a king to death.

The mighty hand leads to a sloping shoulder,
The finger joints are cramped with chalk ;
A goose's quill has put an end to murder
That put an end to talk.

The hand that signed the treaty bred a fever,
And famine grew, and locusts came ;
Great is the hand that holds dominion over
Man by a scribbled name.

The five kings count the dead but do not soften
The crusted wound nor pat the brow ;
A hand rules pity as a hand rules heaven ;
Hands have no tears to flow.

Dylan Thomas.

101. A SWITCH CUT IN APRIL

THIS thin elastic stick was plucked
        From gradual growing in a hedge,
Where early mist awakened leaf,
And late damp hands with spiral stroke
Smoothed slumber from the weighted day,
While flowers drooped with colours furled.

I cut quick circles with the stick :
It whistles in the April air
An eager song, a bugle call,
A signal for the running feet,
For rising flyer flashing sun,
And windy tree with surging crest.

This pliant wood like expert whip
Snaps action in its voice, commands
A quiver from the sloth, achieves
A jerk in buds ; with stinging lash
A spring of movement in the stiff
And sleeping limbs of winter land.

Stick plucked and peeled, companions lost,
Torn from its rooted stock : I hold
Elate and lithe within my hand

Winged answer to the wings' impulse,
The calyx breaking into flame,
The crystal cast into the light.

Clifford Dyment.

102. WAITING

Here at the frozen crossroads of the city,
    Waiting for the lights to call me on,
I think of all the rooms that people wait in
Who watch their waiting hour become a day:
Those villages that wait upon a letter
Where a postman's nod can shrivel up the sun,
Those stations where the wind is an express,
An eager ghost of trains that never come—
Those rooms are only one room, they are mine,
And mine all those dilations of the heart.
I pace about on everybody's heel,
Suspect your knock at every creaking stair,
Take up a book to stave a minute off
And toy with time's impatience in my chair.
The words I read, bewitched upon the page,
Are asking, Is it she and Is it she . . .
But GO the lights now signal, and I go,
And whether you'd have knocked I'll never know.

Alan Hodge.

103. THE UNATTAINED

On the evening of a day on the threshold of Summer,
    Before the full blast of vertiginous Summer, I flung
This foursquare body down upon the crumpled ground,

Moist with a dew-like sweat ; and on all sides heard
The ceaseless clicking and fret of insect swarms ;
I felt energy drain from these limbs spread cruciform,
Dribble away like sap from crushed bracken's veins ;
Felt this my heaviness upon acid-green grass and sand,
Under the passive sky, becoming magnetic as stone ;
And my lids slid down over eyes fanned by coloured
     winds.

And fierce desires swelled up from out my quiet :
To pierce through this flesh outwards, to embrace
The eternal blue, against my nostrils to smother
The fragrant cotton of the clouds ; to feel beneath
The firmly planted and hard soles of feet the grit
Of gravel, the sharp sides of stones ; and endlessly
Against the eyeballs' skin to press fresh images,
To lave in the swift stream of forms these avid eyes :
By passion suspended, hands stretched out, gnawed
From within, O how and to where could I pass ?

Not within facile grasp swings that unattainable
     globe :
Tho' to catch an echo of the spheres' music these ears
     strain
And nostrils yearn for the rich scent of flame and of
     blood,
Hands strive clumsily phantoms' ambiguous flesh to
     caress,
In vain the inward divinity batters against the gates,
Kicking against the pricks until the urgent spirit
     breaks.

Hourly the ocean, World's clock, smashes against the
　　cliffs ;
And savage relentless Time shreds onwards through
　　the skull,
Whispers, " Come home, only Death burns out there."
　　And I know
That this is my body, my shell, and that I am alone
　　and prone.

David Gascoyne.

104.　ORPHEUS IN THE UNDERWORLD

CURTAINS of rock
　　And tears of stone,
Wet leaves in a high crevice of the sky :
From side to side the draperies
Drawn back by rigid hands.

And he came carrying the broken lyre,
And wearing the blue robes of a king,
And looking through eyes like holes torn in a screen ;
And the distant sea was faintly heard,
From time to time, in the suddenly rising wind,
Like broken song.

Out of his sleep, from time to time,
From between half-open lips,
Escape the bewildered words which try to tell
The tale of his bright night
And his wing-shadowed day,
The soaring flights of thought beneath the sun

Above the islands of the seas,
And all the deserts, all the pastures, all the plains
Of the distracting foreign land.

He sleeps with the broken lyre between his hands,
And round his slumber are drawn back
The rigid draperies, the tears and wet leaves,
Cold curtains of rock concealing the bottomless sky.
                                        David Gascoyne.

COMMENTARY

HOPKINS, GERARD MANLEY (1844–1889), the eldest of eight, was born at Stratford, Essex. His father was Consul-General of the Hawaiian Islands to Great Britain, and his mother came from an artistic family. Gerard loved music and drawing. He was educated at Highgate (the school of Lamb, Keats and Coleridge) and at Balliol College, Oxford. In 1866 he became a Roman Catholic, and two years later began his Jesuit training. He preached and ministered, and then taught classics. But he was never strong and he succumbed to typhoid fever at the comparatively early age of 45 years.

His *Poems* were not published until 1918, as Bridges, his friend and literary executor, considered the public was not ready for them, but he released a few poems for anthologies before this date. *The Poems* have had, and are having, a great influence on modern poetry. Is there any other poet who so strongly gives us the sensation that he is present and talking to us ? Talking ; his poetry must be spoken ; it follows the rhythms of current speech. It is here, particularly, that its influence is marked.

Dearest Bridges (p. xvi of Introduction).—This passage refers to *Tom's Garland*, and occurs in *Letters to R. Bridges*, I, 272. Hopkins continually stressed this advice, especially for the more difficult poems. Of *The Leaden Echo and the Golden Echo* he wrote : " The long lines are not rhythm run to seed : everything is weighed and timed in them. Wait till they have taken hold of your ear and you will find it so " (October 18, 1882, I, 155–6).   Of *Harry Ploughman*, the fellow-poem to *Tom's Garland*, he declared that it " is altogether for recital, and not for perusal."

" Sprung rhythm."—Hopkins's eagerness to express thoughts and feelings hardly recognised and sensations unusually keen even for a poet forced him to search for new methods.   His " sprung rhythm " largely solved his problem.   In its closeness to the rhythms of current speech (and of nursery rhymes) and in its flexibility due to the poet's freedom to mass or to separate the accents, and to assemble as many syllables as he requires, it is a powerful instrument in the hands of one capable of controlling it.

He rightly declared it " the most rhetorical and emphatic of all possible rhythms." Its effect is reinforced by an admirable use of alliteration.   This is so organic in Hopkins's work that though it points the meaning and enriches the texture, it is almost unnoticed.

The only thing strange about this metre is the name. For it is the metre of Anglo-Saxon poetry, which was based on accent and linked by alliteration, and never forgotten, though our metre since has been based on time.

In " sprung rhythm " the feet are of equal length, and where they seem unequal pause makes up the difference.   So much is common to our regular metre. But syllabification is different ; a foot may have one to four syllables, and for special effects, any number of weak syllables (as in *The Leaden Echo and the Golden Echo*) : it has one stress, " on the only syllable if there is only one, or, if more, on the first."   Any two stresses may follow upon one another, or be divided by one, two, or three weak syllables.   One licence is characteristic ; *outrides* or *hangers* are one, two, or three syllables sometimes placed before the main stress at the beginning of the foot, and they are not reckoned in the scansion.

1. *The Windhover.*—What Hopkins called "the best thing I ever wrote," is in magnificently successful " sprung rhythm."   Could any other metre so exactly give us the very hovering and dipping of the kestrel's flight, swift and clean-cut, give us as well the sympathy between poet and bird, the empathy [1] in the reader as he follows both ?

The picture of the bird flying, the air, the sun, the strong winds, a skater sweeping round curves !   In his monologue the poet pays grateful tribute to the unconscious perfection of the display by the extraordinary speed and flexibility of his metre.   He then universalises his theme and the monologue is revealed as a dialogue distributed variously, according to the interpretation followed, between Christ, the poet, and the bird.   The whole meaning may include a favourite idea of the poet, the beauty disengaged as the creature, man, poet, bird, is absorbed in fulfilling his characteristic activity.   This is the central motive in, for example, *As Kingfishers Catch Fire*, and in *In Honour of St. Alphonsus Rodriguez* (" Honour is flashed off exploit, so we say ").

It is probable that this poem has been more discussed than any other in Hopkins's work.   There is general agreement that **ah my dear** is addressed to Christ, the poet here following Herbert :

> " I, the unkind ungrateful ?   Ah, my dear,
> I cannot look on Thee."

The first crux is **My heart in hiding** ; the second, the relevance of **here, then** and **chevalier** ; the third and chief one, the last three lines, particularly the last.   I will give first an interpretation, affecting the whole poem, suggested to me by my friend Mrs. Eric Crozier, that the last line might refer to the Crucifixion.

[1] " The power of entering into the experience of or understanding objects or emotions outside ourselves. 1928, ' Rebecca West,' *Strange Necessity*, p. 102.   The active power of empathy which makes the creative artist, or the passive power of empathy which makes the appreciator of art."   (*O.E.D.*)

Searching throughout Hopkins's poetry for the forceful verbs in *The Windhover*, I found in no. 49 a passage strongly supporting this suggestion. Thus the weightiness of this line balances the unique dedication. And if it is adopted, the other difficulties seem to vanish.

" My heart in hiding " (utterly devoted to my vocation) is profoundly moved at the mastery of the bird. A very simple example may make clearer the position adopted here. You may be walking home one evening when there is a magnificent sunset. But you are so excited, it may be, or so deeply engaged on some problem that you miss it, until just as your door is opening you catch a glimpse, and deeply stirred, you turn and watch the sight.

We know, from almost every poem and every letter, that Hopkins's life was " hid with Christ." We know, too, how strong was his love of nature from his drawings as well as his writings.

When these two aspects meet, the physical beauty, great as it was, crumples up in presence of the spiritual passion, which is a billion times greater, that breaks from Thee then, O my Lord. How plain it is : hard toil makes the plough gleam as it goes down the furrow, and Thy dying body, ah my dear, in its very agony, releases dazzling beauty.

This account depends upon the following points :
(*a*) The comparison between the *physical* and *spiritual* is the subject of the whole, as suggested above. It is first stated at the end of the octave, when the poet's spiritual depths are stirred by the physical achievement of the bird.

It is twice repeated in the sestet. First, the physical beauty of the bird (**buckle** is taken in its three meanings, enclose, set to, collapse) crumples up before the spiritual beauty of Christ, who is continually in the poet's mind. Then the gleaming plough, the climax of the ploughman's toil, is contrasted with a symbol of

the climax of Christ's task, fitly concluding the poem
dedicated " To Christ our Lord."
(*b*) That the last line and a half symbolise the Cruci-
fixion is suggested by the identical use of those impres-
sive verbs, gall, gash in Hopkins's no. 49, *In honour
of St. Alphonsus Rodriguez*, where they are used, and
used together, to express the torture or crucifixion of
Christ and the martyrs.

> Honour is flashed off exploit, so we say ;
> And those strokes once, that gashed flesh or galled shield
> Should tongue that time now, trumpet now that field,
> And, on the fighter forge his glorious day
> On Christ they do and on the martyr may.

Other interpretations are those of William Empson,
who compares the bird's active beauty with the
poet's " spiritual renunciation " : " ' in hiding ' implies
the more dangerous life is the windhover's. . . .
The last three lines insist it is no wonder that the [poet's]
life of renunciation should be the more lovely. . . .
' Chevalier ' personifies either Christ riding to Jerus-
alem, . . . ; Pegasus or the Windhover." (*Seven Types
of Ambiguity*, p. 255.) ; of Miss E. E. Phare, who
takes the wood-fire to represent " the condition
of the poet himself." Because " all creatures are
at their loveliest when exerting all their faculties
to the utmost," " to Christ the kestrel is no lovelier
than the sight of the dying fire." (pp. 35–6.) For
fuller details, see her *The Poetry of Gerard Manley
Hopkins*, 1933 ; of Herbert Read, *Twentieth Century
Critical Essays* ; of Dr. I. A. Richards, whose inter-
pretation seems to take the least account of Hopkins's
own point of view, for he considers " in hiding " to mean
" from the life of the senses, from the life of imagination
and emotional risk, from speculation." The last two
lines he interprets " as fuel to his own spirit he (the
poet) has forgotten to burn. . . . The word ' gall '
brings out painfully the shock with which the sight of

the soaring bird has jarred the poet into an unappeased discontent."   (*The Dial* (Chicago) Sept. 19, 1926.)

2. *Heaven-Haven.*—This, one of his loveliest poems, is in regular metre : its melodic curves marked by delicate use of alliteration and the gentler consonants belong as well, unmistakably, to Hopkins's style.   It is interesting to compare these two stanzas with six others called *Rest* (printed in *The Note-Books of G. M. Hopkins*, 1936), for one can see how he worked them over until the perfect version was achieved.

3. *Hurrahing in Harvest.*—In a letter to Bridges (July 6, 1878), the poet wrote " The Hurrahing Sonnet was the outcome of half an hour of extreme enthusiasm as I walked home one day from fishing in the Elwy."   As a sight " of memorable pomp " in nature seems to demand a friend with whom to share the joy, so Hopkins seeks to share his with his greatest Friend.   He was continually striving for assurance of the presence of Christ.

In *A Survey of Modernist Poetry*, Laura Riding and Robert Graves give an illuminating comment on **as a stallion stalwart, very-violet-sweet**, which they interpret " a phrase reconciling the two seemingly opposed qualities of mountains, their male, animal-like roughness and strength and at the same time their ethereal quality under soft light for which the violet in the gentle eye of the horse makes the exactly proper association."

4. *Carrion Comfort* (the title being supplied by Bridges) and 5.   *No worst, there is none . . .* belong to what have been called the terrible sonnets, nos. 32, 40, 41, 45.   They recall the Book of Job ; their content and scope are probably greater than that of any previous sonnets.   The technical mastery in these sonnets, where Hopkins wrests language to do his urgent bidding, is a mine of stimulating innovation.

Carrion Comfort is Hopkins's *Hound of Heaven*, but it is concentrated beyond comparison.   He looks back on the **now done darkness** when he **wretch lay wrestling with (my God !) my God.**

5. *No worst, there is none . . .*, a sonnet ranging problems which beset Shakespeare and Milton at their most serious, contains no consolation. Sleep and death remain. In this, one of his greatest poems, the dramatic structure present in most of his sonnets—as very generally in his poetry—is particularly poignant ; hopelessness, lamentation, envisaging of desperate problems—these yet present a passionate unity. The passage **O the mind, mind has mountains . . . steep or deep** has the power and compression of Shakespeare. F. R. Leavis brings unquestionable examples to show the affinity,

the world-without-end hour

or

If it were done when 'tis done . . .

Cf. *New Bearings in English Poetry*, 1932.

HOUSMAN, ALFRED EDWARD (1859–1935), was educated at Bromsgrove School and St. John's College, Oxford, of which later he became an Honorary Fellow. He first entered the Civil Service, in the Patent Office, and then became Professor of Latin at University College, London, from 1892 to 1911. In the latter year he went to Cambridge, where he was to remain, as Professor of Latin and Fellow of Trinity College. *The Shropshire Lad* was published in 1896, *Last Poems* in 1922, and happily, *More Poems*, edited by his brother Laurence in 1936. A few more poems and light verse are included in *A.E.H.: Some Poems, Letters, Personal Memoir*, by his brother Laurence Housman, 1937. Some of his scholarship is preserved in his exhaustive critical edition of Manilius and Juvenal ; as well as in his many articles in the *Classical Review*, the *Classical Quarterly*, and the *Journal of Philology*.

6. *When green buds hang in the elm like dust . . .* is one of the best in *More Poems*. It is pleasant to meet this note of vitality in his last volume.

YEATS, WILLIAM BUTLER, was born in 1865 at Sandymount near Dublin, and was educated at the Godolphin School, Hammersmith, and the Erasmus School, Dublin ; for a time he studied painting at his father's request, but gave it up. He was a Senator of the Irish Free State 1922–8. The Nobel Prize for Literature was awarded to him in 1923. He has honorary doctorates of Oxford, Cambridge and Dublin.

About 1899, with Lady Gregory and others, he founded the Abbey Theatre. His plays were produced there. He helped the national drama further by discovering Synge in Paris and getting him to return to Ireland and write plays for the Abbey Theatre.

Among his publications are *Plays for an Irish Theatre*, 1913 ; *Autobiographies*, 1926 ; *Collected Poems*, 1933 ; *Wheels and Butterflies, New Plays*, 1934 ; *Full Moon in March*, 1935 ; *Dramatis Personæ*, 1936.

7. *The Cat and the Moon* was sung by the First Musician, in the play so-called, first performed at the Abbey Theatre on May 9, 1926. Stanza one begins the play, stanza two is sung as the Beggars move round the stage, and the third is sung at the end. The play is in *Wheels and Butterflies*. The poem was printed first in *The Wild Swans at Coole* (1919), and in *Collected Poems*, 1933.

8. *Sailing to Byzantium* occurs in *The Tower*, 1928 and

9. *Byzantium* in *The Winding Stair*, 1933. These two belong together ; for in the first poem the poet contrasts the ephemerality of man with the permanence of art and resolves when " once out of nature " to assume such a form as that of the golden bird that Greek artificers made for the Emperor of Byzantium : in the splendid *Byzantium* he gives a fresh vision of the miraculous life of art : the great cathedral of St^{a.} Sophia, the glory of the golden bird, the Emperor's gold and marble mosaic pavements spirit-haunted. These are an unending contrast to the struggles and confusion of humanity.

Byzantium is an exciting name in the history of art. For eleven centuries from the time of the Emperor Constantine the Great who made Byzantium a capital in A.D. 324 until 1453, the Byzantines, centred in Constantinople, closed the door against the hordes of Asia, and cultivated a remarkable technique in painting and mosaic. They used the most splendid materials in their art for they were enormously wealthy. St^{a.} Sophia gloriously embodies the surviving monuments.

8. *Sailing to Byzantium.*

perne in a gyre : gyre, a spiral, here seems to represent the twisting, twirling flames, the perne, the core of stillness. (cf. Yeats' *Collected Poems*, p. 445, pern—spool.)   perne is usually spelt *pirn*, a Scots word meaning spool or bobbin, also spinning-top ; often used in proverbial phrases, e.g. " I shall have a fine ravelled pirn to unwind." (R. L. Stevenson, *Catriona*, chap. xxiii.)

The stanza refers to the martyrs on the one side (on the other Virgins) in a wonderful and terrible Byzantium mosaic forming a great frieze on the walls of S. Apollinare Nuovo in Ravenna, 560 B.C.   Thus; may these saintly presences come from the fire of their martyrdom, still and resolute amid the whirl of flame, and teach my soul their divine music.

a form . . . make : this is an artificial golden singing-bird. Compare Yeats' own note : " I have read somewhere that in the Emperor's palace at Byzantium was a tree made of gold and silver, and artificial birds that sang." (*Collected Poems*, p. 446.)   Such birds were well known. (See Marlowe, *Hero and Leander*, sestiad 1, II. 31-6.)

9. *Byzantium.*

Hades' bobbin : a spirit. Blood-begotten spirits, probably human ghosts who, haunting the flame-mosaic pavement, are purged of their complexities of fury by its grandeur. The phrase describing them is a parenthesis, so that the account of the flames begotten of flame continues as Dying into a dance.

dolphin : Mr. Yeats tells me " I certainly got the idea of the dolphins carrying souls to Paradise from a book on Roman sculpture."

10. *A Dialogue of Self and Soul.*   This fine and courageous poem is itself complementary to the Byzantium poems.   These express the appeal and the refuge of art : the *Dialogue* expresses the determination not to escape, but to face all that life can bring.   Marvell's *A Dialogue between the Soul and Body* is interesting in its difference :

> O who shall from this Dungeon raise
> A Soul inslav'd so many wayes ?

Sato : A common surname in Japan.

Montashigi : Dr. Giles tells me nothing is known of this.

MEW, CHARLOTTE MARY (1870–1928), was born in London.   All her life was a wavering struggle with illness and financial difficulties.   It is some comfort to think that many friends appreciated her " passionate sincerity " and loyalty as well as her charm and wit.

Her father was an architect but he died when she was a child and her mother, two sisters and brother were unable to cope with the troubles that haunted their days.   Three of her early works were published by Aubrey Beardsley in the *Yellow Book* the first, her short story *Passed* and then two essays, on Charlotte Brontë and on *Trees.*

She lived always in Bloomsbury, and this was fortunate, for in connexion with Harold Monro's Poetry Bookshop she experienced some of her happiest days.   Her work was welcomed and published there and Alida Klementaski (Mrs. Harold Monro) became one of her greatest friends.

In 1922, Thomas Hardy (who thought highly of her work, and had invited her to Max Gate), John Masefield, and Walter de la Mare, with Mr. Baldwin's help, procured a Civil List pension for her. When her mother died and in 1927 her sister, after great suffering, died too, she seemed to lose all interest in life, and herself died in 1928.

She published *The Farmer's Bride* in 1915. *The Rambling Sailor*, 1929, an attractive small quarto, contains a portrait and a memoir by Alida Monro upon which this account is based. Nos. 11 and 12 both occur in the latter book.

DE LA MARE, WALTER JOHN (1873), Hon. Litt.D. Cambridge, Professor of Fiction in the Royal Society of Literature, was educated at St. Paul's Cathedral School. His published work includes poetry, fiction and short stories, criticism and highly individual and attractive anthologies. His chief poetical volumes were : *The Listeners*, 1912 ; *Peacock Pie*, 1913 ; *Motley*, 1918 ; *The Veil*, 1921 ; *The Fleeting*, 1933, and a collected edition, *Poems 1901–1918*, in 1920. His fiction includes, in 1904 *Henry Brocken*, in 1910 *The Return* which gained the first Prince Edward de Polignac Prize, and *The Three Mulla-Mulgars*, in 1921 *The Memoirs of a Midget*. *Come Hither*, his chief anthology, was published in 1923.

A biographical and critical study, *Walter de la Mare* by R.-L. Mégroz 1927, *A Bibliography* by the present writer, in *The London Mercury* 1927. A critical study by Forrest Reid, *Walter de la Mare*, 1929. *The Song of Shadows* (and its peer, *The Mad Prince*) in *Peacock Pie* and *The Ghost* in *Motley* are typical of the grace and gentleness in his poetry. The soft lyricism of the first, and the questioning, wondering note in the second, are to be found throughout his poetry.

THOMAS, PHILIP EDWARD (1878–Easter Monday 1917), was educated at St. Paul's School and Lincoln College, Oxford. He served in the Artists' Rifles during the war until he was killed in action in April 1917.

His prose includes works on the English countryside, on Oxford, on Wales, the Isle of Wight and the Icknield Way, a few books of essays, biographical studies of R. Jefferies, M. Maeterlinck, G. Borrow, Lafcadio Hearn, Swinburne and Pater, and various anthologies, and in addition editorial work and many articles in periodicals.

Memoirs are given in *The Tenth Muse*, second edition 1917 by John Freeman, and *As I knew him* by J. W. Haines in *In Memoriam: Edward Thomas*—The Morland Press, 190 Ebury Street, S.W., July 1919. A *Bibliography* by the present writer in *The London Mercury*, 1927, *Edward Thomas*, by Robert P. Eckert, 1937.

It was not till the beginning of the war that Robert Frost suggested Thomas's writing poetry. He began at once and wrote hard until Christmas 1916. His friend, J. W. Haines, writes "Of the 150 poems he told me he had written, a great many were composed in railway trains after it was too dark for him to read and were written down later. He frequently altered them." His first volume, *Six Poems*, 1916, was published under the name of Edward Eastaway, but the others under his own, *Poems* in 1917, and *Last Poems* in 1918. *The Collected Poems*, 1920, contains a foreword of interesting criticism by Walter de la Mare.

Edward Thomas was no Georgian. Like Harold Monro, he is entirely himself. He has some of the social consciousness that is being emphasised to-day; he has extreme delicacy of sensation (" he seemed to me to be able to use all his senses at once more acutely than most people use a single one," J. W. Haines); and, more rare, he has magic too, on " the borders of sleep," " past the edge of the world."

16. *Old Man.*

I cannot like the scent, Yet I would give up others more sweet. Mr. Haines remembers " that, for the whole of the last evening he spent with me, he at intervals pulled some mysterious object out of his pocket to smell. What it was I never saw, but it seemed to give him nearly as much satisfaction as his pipe."

MARQUIS, DON(ALD ROBERT PERRY) (1878–January 1937), was born in Walnut, Illinois. He was married twice. He wrote easily and with imagination and humour. He contributed to newspapers all his life, and his entertaining columns in the *New York Sun* and *New York Tribune* set a standard and brought him great popularity which was accorded also to his light verses and humorous stories. He was himself much interested in his plays, and *The Old Soak* (1921) ran for over a year in New York City.

But his light verse will be longest remembered. And his dramatic qualities find expression here also. In *archy and mehitabel* (1927 U.S.A., 1931 London), his insects and animals are real and human, their dialogue direct and vivid. archy the cockroach was once a vers libre bard and mehitabel the cat was Cleopatra. archy explains the appearance of this verse by saying that he typed at night, just able to work the machine " one slow letter after another," but " could not work the capital letters."

archy's story of *pete the parrot and shakespeare* is amusing ; with *the lesson of the moth*, trying to fry himself on the wires of the electric bulb because

> " it is better to be happy
> for a moment
> and be burned up with beauty,"

archy does not agree, and yet he concludes :

> " but at the same time i wish
> there was something i wanted
> as badly as he wanted to fry himself."

Among Don Marquis's other publications are *Poems and Portraits*, 1922 ; *Love Sonnets of a Cave Man*, 1928 (new verses and some of the best of the early humorous ones) ; *Off the Arm*, 1930 (a novel) ; and *archy does his part*, 1935. A collection of his serious verse, as well as of this lighter kind, is being made for early publication.

I am able to print, through the kindness of his sister, Bernice M. Marquis, the following verses privately printed by her in 1936 after his last illness began.

> I am mine own priest, and I shrive myself
> Of all my wasted yesterdays. Though sin
> And sloth and foolishness, and all ill weeds
> Of error, evil and neglect grow rank
> And ugly there, I dare forgive myself
> That error, sin, sloth and foolishness.
> God knows that yesterday I played the fool ;
> God knows that yesterday I played the knave ;
> But shall I therefore cloud this new dawn o'er
> With fog of futile sighs and vain regrets ?
>
> This is another day ; and its young strength
> Is laid upon the quivering hills until,
> Like Egypt's Memnon, they grow quick with song.
> This is another day, and the bold world
> Leaps up and grasps its light, and laughs, as leapt
> Prometheus up and wrenched the fire from Zeus.
>
> This is another day—are its eyes blurred
> With maudlin grief for any wasted past ?
> A thousand thousand failures shall not daunt !
> And out of all the dust and death of mine
> Old selves I dare to lift a singing heart
> And living faith ; my spirit dares drink deep
> Of the red mirth mantling in the cup of morn.

19. *the old trouper.*

richard mansfield : Richard Mansfield (1854–1907) represented the romantic tradition of acting, " the grand style " in plays and playing ; he was famous too for his " modern " playing of Shaw's Comedies. He is said to have been the first in America to recognise their quality. It was chance got him first, after much endeavour, into spoken drama : he told the actors he would be famous tomorrow night, and he was ! Dr.

Jekyll and Mr. Hyde and Peer Gynt were his most famous rôles.

mr booth : Edwin Booth (1833–1893), influenced by the Kean tradition, was a famous tragedian. Richelieu was his favourite rôle. In 1878 he published *Edwin Booth's Prompt Book*, which contained the text of fifteen of his usual plays, chiefly Shakespearean. It is well known to students of drama. Some of his interpretations are quoted in the Variorum edition of *Othello* and the *Merchant of Venice*.

mr daly : John Augustin Daly (1838–1899) was a well-known playwright and producer. " He demanded of his company the loyalty he gave them." He wrote or adapted about 90 plays.

jo jefferson : Joseph Jefferson (1829–1905) was one of the best-loved of American actors, and was on the stage for 71 years, having begun at the age of 4. He supported his family at 13, when his father died. Then, for years he wished to play Rip van Winkle, and at last having got Dion Boucicault to write a new version of it, he played it so successfully that " every American child was taken to see it."

modjeska : Helena Modjeska (1840–1909) was a Polish-American actress, born in Cracow. She went to America in 1876, and learned English in six months, at the bidding of Edwin Booth. She played heroines of Shakespeare, and produced as well.

For fuller details see the *Dictionary of American Biography*, to which I am indebted.

LINDSAY, NICHOLAS VACHEL (1879–1931) was educated at Springfield High School and Hiram College, Ohio, at the Art Institute, Chicago, and the New York School of Art. He married in 1925 and had two children. He lectured for the Y.M.C.A. and the Anti Saloon League, 1905–10, and then used to walk and tramp, from Illinois to New Mexico and through the southern states distributing " Rhymes to be Traded for

Bread " to the farmers, and speaking of " The Gospel of Beauty."   He used to recite and chant his poems before many schools, universities, and other institutions in America and England. His publications include, in verse : *General William Booth enters into Heaven and Other Poems*, 1913 ; *The Congo, and Other Poems*, 1914 ; *The Chinese Nightingale*, 1920 ; *Collected Poems*, 1923 ; *Collected Poems* (illustrated by self), 1925 ; *Johnny Appleseed and Other Poems for Children*, 1928 ; *Selected Poems*, 1931 ; in prose : *A Handy Guide for Beggars*, 1916 ; *Adventures while Preaching the Gospel of Beauty*, 1914 ; *The Art of the Moving Picture*, 1915 ; *Going to the Sun* (drawings), 1923 ; *The Litany of Washington Street*, 1929.

20. *General William Booth* . . .—This poem was written " to the tune of ' The Blood of the Lamb ' with indicated instruments," and even without a band it was a stimulating experience to listen to Harold Monro declaiming it at one of the Readings of the Poetry Bookshop, and even more exciting to hear Vachel Lindsay himself.

It is a processional poem ; the sense of crowding and the blare of the trumpets are suggested in the rhetorical rhythms. The contrast here with the simplicity with which the story is told produces a great effect. " Adventures while Singing these Songs," the Introduction to his *Collected Poems*, casts an interesting light on Lindsay's conception of his poetry.

William Booth (1829–1912), the founder of the Salvation Army, was operated on for cataract in 1908, and finally became blind in the year of his death. Cf. *God's Soldier* (1934), by St. John Ervine, and *Life of William Booth* (1920), by Harold Begbie.

MONRO, HAROLD (1879–1932), was born in Brussels, where he lived till he was seven, then was taken to Wells, Somerset. He was educated at Radley School and Caius College, Cambridge. For some years he seemed moody and restless and changed occupation and place ; a land agent in Ireland, next founding a short-lived private press, the Samurai, at Haslemere, then living on the Continent. At Florence, stimulated by Maurice Hewlett, he determined to carry out his own idea of trying to improve the conditions of English poetry. So he returned and ran his *Poetry Review* during 1912, and in 1913 founded the Poetry Bookshop in Devonshire Street. The " shop " became widely known and its poetry readings, at which poets read their own works, or Monro and Alida Klementaski read the works of others, had widespread influence. His magazine *Poetry and Drama* appeared 1913–14. In the war Monro was on duty in the War Office. He married Alida Klementaski in 1920. *The Chapbook*, his most interesting periodical, began in July 1919, and was stopped in October 1925 to the regret of its readers. His most important book now is : *The Collected Poems* (1933), edited by Alida Monro with a biographical sketch by F. S. Flint and a critical note by T. S. Eliot.

Monro published the volumes of *Georgian Poetry*, but he was always himself rather than a Georgian. His work does not lose by collection, unlike that of some of his best-known contemporaries. Though he invented little in the way of technique, he is otherwise thoughtful and original.

22. *Clock*—In view of Einstein's work, it is perhaps not remarkable how many poems since the war deal with some aspect of time.

23. *Real Property*.—This is not " nature-poetry," but the townsman's dream of the country.

FREEMAN, JOHN (1880–1929), was born in London. He married Gertrude Farren in 1902 and they had two daughters. It became known to the literary world after Freeman's death how distinguished had been his place in the busy life of the City, where he was Chief Executive Officer of the Liverpool Victoria Friendly Society. His gifts for psychological insight and for organisation, amply evident in work of such magnitude, are not less notable in his writing, in his poetry as well as in his criticism.

Three of his books especially make him known, his *Letters* and the two collected volumes of poetry. *John Freeman's Letters*, edited by Gertrude Freeman and Sir John Squire, with an Introduction by W. de la Mare (1936), show us, most humanly and with charm, the man and the poet, and, incidentally, the critic. *Collected Poems*, with a portrait by Laura Knight (1928), and *Last Poems*, with an Introduction by Sir John Squire, and a photograph (1930), show how individual and how varied was his gift for poetry.

Among his other publications, in prose, were *Portrait of George Moore*, 1922 ; *English Portraits and Essays*, 1924 ; *Herman Melville*, 1926 ; in poetry, *Memories of Childhood*, 1918 and 1919 ; *Poems New and Old*, 1920 (the Hawthornden Prize being awarded to him this year); *Music : Lyrical and Narrative Poems*, 1921 ; *Prince Absalom*, 1925 ; *Solomon and Balkis*, 1926 ; and the two volumes mentioned above.

25. *Rhymeless* comes from *Last Poems*.

ASQUITH, THE HON. HERBERT (1881), the eldest surviving son of the first Earl of Oxford and Asquith, was educated at Winchester and Balliol College, Oxford, and at Lincoln's Inn, and was called to the bar in 1907.   He served in the war in France and Flanders, 1915–18, as a captain in the R.F.A.

His poems have been published in three volumes, in *The Volunteer*, 1915 ; *A Village Sermon*, 1920 ; and a collected volume, *Poems*, 1934.   Among his other publications are the following novels : *Wind's End*, 1924 ; *Young Orlando*, 1927 ; *Roon*, 1929 ; *Mary Dallon*, 1932.

26. *Nightfall* comes from *Poems*, 1934.

POUND, EZRA LOOMIS (1885), of English descent, was born in Idaho, and educated at Hamilton College and the University of Pennsylvania. In 1907 he travelled in Spain, Italy and Provence, while seeking for material for a thesis on Lope de Vega. He lived in Venice and then for ten years in London, where he translated, wrote and lectured in the interests of the new poetry. Carl Sandburg pointed out " he has done most of living men to incite new impulses in poetry . . .," due to the strong desire to rouse and fire other minds. For his important work in connexion with Imagism, see under H. D.

In 1914 he married. Later, he went to Paris for four years, and then settled in Rapallo on the Italian Riviera.

His published works include *Personæ*, and *Exultations*, 1909 ; *Ripostes*, 1912 ; *Lustra*, 1916 ; *Hugh Selwyn Mauberley*, 1920 ; *Collected Poems*, 1926 [1927] ; *Selected Poems* (Faber Library), 1928 ; *A Draft of XXX Cantos 1933*.

27. *The Return* appeared in *Ripostes*. This is widely recognised as one of the finest poems that Pound has written.

They return: this seems to refer to the Furies, Mercury and the hounds of Diana. These lines might have been written to suggest the questing of the Furies, as in a recent representation of Orestes, though, of course, the poem was actually published long before.

28. *Envoi 1919* occurs in *Hugh Selwyn Mauberley*.

thou : the book.

in thee : in the book.

29. *Kung's Wisdom* from *Canto XIII*.

A Reader and Speakers can dramatise this disputation very effectively.

bo leaves : the bo tree is the name given in Ceylon to the Pipal tree, reverenced by the Buddhists because the Buddha sat under it to teach. *The Life and Teachings of Confucius*, by J. Legge (Vol. I of the Chinese Classics), 1809, is still the standard authority on Confucianism.

LAWRENCE, DAVID HERBERT (1885–1931), was born in Eastwood, Nottinghamshire, the son of a miner. He was educated at Nottingham High School and later at Nottingham University College, where he both wrote his first novel, *The White Peacock*, and qualified as a teacher. For two years he taught in Croydon and then began to earn his living as a writer. He married in 1914 and after the war travelled widely. His *Letters* (edited by Aldous Huxley, 1932) are an interesting autobiography in little. He wrote many novels, short stories, and travel sketches : his poetry was collected in 1932.

30. *Sphinx* appears in *The Imagist Anthology* : 31. *Green*, and 33. *Mountain Lion* in the *Collected Poems* : 32. *Work* in *Pansies*, 1929.

32. *Work* seems to be a crystallisation of Lawrence's life-long attitude to work. To identify oneself with the job in hand, to be its spirit as it were and to try to realise this as perfectly as a tree clothes itself in foliage. A comment by Aldous Huxley (*Letters*, p. xxxi) illustrates this point : " One of the great charms of Lawrence as a companion was that he could never be bored and so could never be boring. He was able to absorb himself completely in what he was doing at the moment ; and he regarded no task as too humble for him to undertake, nor so trivial that it was not worth his while to do it well."

33. *Mountain Lion.*—By some instinct the poet seemed to understand the "feelings" of plants or animals, as well as he knew their appearance and the impression they made. Here he has that sympathy with the lion that he shows also in *Snake* (perhaps his most-quoted poem), and that the unknown Chinese painter had with the Tiger in his great picture in the British Museum, so that we see the animal as it sees itself, or as Blake saw it.

¿ Qué tiene, amigo, León ? : What are you holding, friend, a lion ?

Hermoso s ! : Either : It is beautiful ! or, oh you beauty !

CORNFORD, FRANCES (1886), was born at Cambridge. Her father was Sir Francis Darwin, and her grandfather, Charles Darwin ; her mother was Ellen Wordsworth Crofts, a lecturer at Newnham College. She was educated privately, and married Francis Macdonald Cornford, Fellow and Classical Lecturer of Trinity College, Cambridge.

Her publications include *Spring Morning*, 1915 ; *Different Days*, 1928; and *Mountains and Molehills*, with woodcuts by Gwen Raverat, 1934, from which *On August Thirteenth* and *Grand Ballet* are chosen.

36. *Grand Ballet.*

like an escapèd dove : Nijinsky was famous among dancers for his power of apparently flying through the air. See *Nijinsky*, by Romola Nijinsky, 1933, and *The Tragedy of Nijinsky*, by Anatole Bournan and D. Lyman, 1937. Actually the phrase applies chiefly to that **one immortal moment**.

H. D., as she wishes to be called, was born at Bethlehem, Pennsylvania, in 1886. In 1904 she entered Bryn Mawr College, in 1911 visited Italy and France, and London, where Ezra Pound encouraged her in her poetry. She married Richard Aldington in 1913. Her publications include *Sea Garden*, 1916 ; *Choruses from the Iphigenia in Aulis and the Hippolytus of Euripides*, 1919 ; *Hymen*, 1921 (lyrics) ; *Heliodora and other Poems*, 1924 ; *Collected Poems of H. D.*, 1925 ; *Hippolytus Temporizes*, 1927 (verse play).

H. D. was one of the leading Imagists ; it was they, with Wilfred Owen, Pound, Eliot, and Hopkins, whose work in its many transformations and experiments prepared the way for post-war poetry right up to the present date. T. E. Hulme (1883–killed in action 1917) can be described as the father of the movement. His five short poems were less important than his stimulating talk and discussions (first in 1908), represented in his later *Speculations* (1924), in which he proclaimed that at the end of a period of romanticism a new technique was needed, with accurate presentation and no verbiage.   In 1909, Ezra Pound joined him and named the group 'Des Imagistes,' and he was the driving force behind their first anthology, *Des Imagistes* (1914). He had already in *A Few Don'ts by an Imagiste* (*Poetry*, Chicago, March 1913) presented in incisive and stirring language the reforms he had been practising himself.

Amy Lowell then arranged the next three anthologies in 1915, '16 and '17.   In these the ' official imagists ' were Richard Aldington, H. D., J. G. Fletcher, F. S. Flint, D. H. Lawrence, and Amy Lowell.   In the 1915 volume was their famous credo, and this clearly implied what they were reacting against.   It ran :

(*a*) To use the language of common speech, but the *exact* word, not the nearly exact, nor the merely decorative word.

(*b*) To create new rhythms as the expressions of new moods.

(*c*) To allow absolute freedom in subject.   It is not good art to write badly about aeroplanes and automobiles ; nor is it necessarily bad art to write well about the past.

(*d*) To present an image.   Poetry should render particulars exactly, and not deal in vague generalities, however magnificent and sonorous.   It is for this reason we oppose the ' cosmic ' poet.

(*e*) To produce poetry that is hard and clear, never blurred nor indefinite.

(*f*) Concentration is of the very essence of poetry.

37. *Chance Meeting* appeared in the *Imagist Anthology* 1930, and is reprinted in H. D.'s attractive collection, *Red Roses for Bronze*, 1931.

38. *I would forgo* . . . . is no. 111 of the Choros Sequence from *Morpheus* " Dream-dark-winged."   H. D. is fond of Switzerland and often spends a few months there, but, as she writes to me, " My main interest, as you

know, has been in trying to bring to people something of the clarity and beauty not only of ancient but of modern Greece."

WYLIE, ELINOR (1887–1928), was born in New Jersey, the daughter of Henry Hoyt, Solicitor-General in the administration of Theodore Roosevelt. She became fond of travel, and lived abroad for some time, particularly in England, both in Chelsea and the country. In 1921 her *Nets to Catch the Wind* was widely welcomed. Most of her writing was accomplished after her marriage to William Rose Benét in 1923, though she continued to use her previous married name on her books. She published four novels and the following books of poems : *Black Armour* (1923), *Trivial Breath* (1928), and her finest work in the posthumous volume, *Angels and Earthly Creatures* (1929). Her *Collected Poems*, with a Foreword by William Rose Benét, appeared in 1932.

The best criticism to date on her work is in Louis Untermeyer's *Modern American Poetry* (1932), and in Harriet Monroe's *Poets and their Art* (1932). Untermeyer's volume has a good selection from her work, and includes *Velvet Shoes*, in which snow-silence is delicately suggested, in " its soundless space " and " its windless peace."

39. *O Virtuous Light* is taken from *Collected Poems*.
The instrument of reason failed : the intuition which threatens the senses is not a light by which to live.

MUIR, EDWIN, was born in Orkney in 1887, and educated at the Kirkwall Burgh School. After work in shipbuilding offices on the Clyde, he became a journalist, translator (especially of German literature) and an author. In 1921 he and his wife moved to Prague, and thence to various countries on the Continent until 1931.

His publications include, in fiction, *The Marionette, The Three Brothers, Poor Tom*; in criticism, *The Structure of the Novel* 1928 ; in biography, *John Knox*; in poetry, *Six Poems* 1931, *Variations on a Time Theme* 1934, and *Journeys and Places* 1937.

40. *The Riders* has been chosen from *Variations on a Time Theme*, and first appeared in *The Listener*.

Mr. Muir writes to me about *The Riders* :
" the point round which the poem crystallised was the beginning :

> At the dead centre of the boundless plain
> Does our way end ?   Our horses pace and pace
> Like steeds forever labouring on a shield.

These lines came to me spontaneously, without my being conscious of the possible development they implied. The development grew from a variety of associations that would have remained isolated and disconnected but for this image, which acted as a sort of magnet, and drew them into a rough pattern round it.   The Horses, as I see them, are an image of human time, the invisible body of humanity on which we ride for a little while, which has come from places we did not know :

> They have borne upon their saddles
> Forms fiercer than the tiger, borne them calmly
> As they bear us now,

and which is going towards places we shall not know :

> Suppliantly
> The rocks will melt, the sealed horizons fall
> Before their onset.

Yet the steed—mankind in its course through time—is mortal, and the rider is immortal.   I stated this belief tentatively in the poem, because it was written in a mood of unusual dejection.   The painful emotion in the poem comes from a simultaneous feeling of immortality and mortality, and particularly from the feeling that we, as immortal spirits, are imprisoned in a very small and from all appearances fortuitously selected length of time : held captive on the 'worn saddle,' which in spite of our belief in our immortality has the power ' to charm us to obliviousness ' by ' the scent of the ancient leather.'

" I was not aware, or at least fully aware, of all these implications when I wrote the poem ; and I have only realised during the last year that almost all my poems from the start have been about journeys and places : that is, about the two sides of the paradox [of mortality and immortality] one of which implies the other."

I was glad to get the following interesting reply from the poet to a query about **the autumn light.**— " I actually saw once, many years ago, the picture as I set it down : it is one of the few things in the poem taken from observation. It was a clear bright day in late autumn down in Sussex : the weight seemed to have left every physical object with the drying up of the leaves still sticking to the trees without burdening them. A boy was ploughing in a field, and a moving column of breath went on before him ; his own breath ; but the air was so light and clear, the picture so distinct, that what my eye saw was the column going in front and the boy following it. Why this struck me so much I can't say yet ; but when I came to this part of the poem it seemed to be the correspondence I needed.

" ' . . . The autumn light/We still remember ' of which the ' coal-black glossy hides ' do not keep a glimmer. I think this is an attempt to suggest those isolated moments of pure vision which have a feeling of timelessness (and are often called timeless). My feeling about these moments (which are a common experience, though most people are unconscious of them) has always been that they do not *go into* Time ; that they do not change the actual physical body of Time, symbolised by the horses. They may cast a momentary reflection on the glossy hides, but it fades almost at once. This instant fading makes them 'autumnal.' At the moment when we are aware of them we are released from the presence of Time : our limbs are 'weightless.' Our silvery breaths going on before us ' Leading our empty bodies through the air ' is an extravagant way of describing this state of freedom."

SITWELL, EDITH, was born at Scarborough in 1887, and educated privately. Among her publications are *The Mother and Other Poems,* 1915 ; *Clown's Houses,* 1918 ; *Bucolic Comedies,* 1923 ; *Troy Park* (poems), 1925 ; *Elegy on Dead Fashion,* 1926 ; *Gold Coast Customs,* 1929 ; *Collected Poems,* 1930 ; *Selected Poems with an Essay on her own Poetry,* 1936 ; *Alexander Pope* (biography), 1930 ; *The Pleasures of Poetry,* an Anthology, 1932 ; *Bath,* 1932 ; *Victoria of England,* 1936 ; *I Live under a Black Sun* (novel), 1937 ; [with Osbert Sitwell] *Twentieth Century Harlequinade, and other Poems,* 1916. Editor of *Wheels,* 1916–1921.

"They issue forth from their bright pavilions, and demand trouble." Arnold Bennett, in 1923, thus happily characterised the three Sitwell poets, if one understands that *demand trouble* is used figuratively to express their artistic revolt against the stereotyped and dull, their championship of individuality (their own) in style and subject.

In deliberate opposition to the Georgian Poetry anthologies, 1911–22, Edith Sitwell, supported by her brothers and other friends, edited *Wheels* 1916–21. Their anthology was influential in many ways, in the encouragement it gave to sympathisers, in the very hostility and scorn it roused in the more traditional ranks. And here, in general stimulation towards experimentation of many kinds and in directions then unknown, lies Edith's and her brothers' importance in the history of this period.

In style, it was particularly Edith Sitwell's extreme skill in technique, in texture, in new images and symbols, in synæsthesia (strange to her readers yet itself old), in liveliness of metre, which suggested that a certain richness might again be possible in English poetry.

It is in the details that she is interesting, rarely in the whole : her isolated conceits, brought together by free association, presented in her pastorals and occasional poems a world of bright surfaces.

But in her satires, especially in *Gold Coast Customs*, she has new symbols, many of them grim, the ironically used figures of the Harlequinade, faintly demoniacal in their bearing, or more terrible, from the jungle, to express her vision of the spiritual death and chaos in much of contemporary life. She is involved in no political creed, she has no nostrum, no remedy at hand. And she flees to the past, to the dream-world of her own youth in *Troy Park* ; and to the elegance and grace of the eighteenth century, both in her poetry and in her prose.

Descent from Parnassus, by Dilys Powell, 1934, contains criticism, and *The Three Sitwells* by R.-L. Mégroz, 1927, is biographical and has useful synopses.

41. *The Little Ghost Who Died for Love* is taken from *Selected Poems*, 1936.

In the Introduction the poet tells us " When my poems deal with emotion, they are always the most simple and primitive emotion of simple and primitive people, as in *The Heart and the Hambone* and *The Little Ghost Who Died for Love*. I write of a dead girl returning to the world in spring."

The cherries : symbolising the spring and the maidens in the moonlit orchard when the dead girl comes back, are a favourite symbol of the poet's. She builds up her " country world," and the bright dream-world of much of her poetry, with fruits, and jewels and the jewel-colours of gold and silver, with apricots, flames-jewel-cold, silver corn ; or with tactile images, bear-dark forests, golden nets of summer light, the purring fire or the moonlight cold as amber.

the apothecary at the Fair . . . doctor's bare Booth . these three terms call up the quacksalver described in Overbury's *Characters* in 1615, for this figure was only too typical, for generations. A lively woodcut was published in 1707, " *The Infallible Mountebank and Quack Doctor,* standing, with Harlequin to support him outside his tent or booth, in the Fair." (Both are printed in *A Cabinet of Characters,* 1925, by the present writer.)

MOORE, MARIANNE, was born in St. Louis, Missouri, in 1887, and was educated at the Metager Institute, Carlisle, Pennsylvania, at Bryn Mawr, and at Carlisle Commercial College. She taught in the U.S. Indian School, Carlisle, and then became an Assistant in New York Public Library, 1921–25. She was Acting Editor of *The Dial,* 1925–29, and received the *Dial* Award for 1924, the Helen Haire Levinson Prize, 1932, and the Ernest Hartsock Memorial Award, 1935. Her publications include : *Poems,* 1921 ; *Observations,* 1924 ; *Selected Poems,* with a critical introduction by T. S. Eliot, 1935 ; *The Pangolin and Other Verse,* 1936. She contributes verse and criticism to such magazines as *The Criterion, The New English Weekly,* and to *Life and Letters To-day,* in this country. Her work was first published in *The Egoist.*

43. *Silence.*

In the lines

> The deepest feeling always shows itself in silence ;
> not in silence, but restraint

the dictum applies admirably to Marianne Moore's own poetry, which is distinguished by strong control, springing from strong emotion.

ELIOT, THOMAS STEARNS, was born in St. Louis, Missouri, in 1888. He was educated at Harvard University, at the Sorbonne in Paris, at Harvard again and then at Merton College, Oxford. In 1927 he became a British subject. His publications include: many reviews, articles and essays in periodicals; poetry, *Prufrock and Other Observations*, 1917; *Poems*, 1919; *The Waste Land* [won the *Dial* Award, 1922], 1922; *Poems 1909–1925* [includes his previous work, and adds *The Hollow Men*, 1925], 1925; *Ash Wednesday*, 1930; *The Rock* (a pageant play), 1934; *Collected Poems 1909–1935*, 1936; criticism, *The Sacred Wood*, 1920; *Homage to John Dryden*, 1924; *For Lancelot Andrewes*, 1928; *Dante*, 1929; *The Use of Poetry*, 1933; *After Strange Gods*, 1934; *Selected Essays 1917–32*, 1935; *Murder in the Cathedral*, 1935.

The most useful books, to date, on T. S. Eliot's poetry are, *The Achievement of T. S. Eliot*, by F. O. Matthiessen, 1935; *Descent from Parnassus*, by Dilys Powell, 1934; *The Poetry of T. S. Eliot*, by H. R. Williamson, 1932.

The history of modern poetry since 1914 cannot be written without emphasising the importance of *Prufrock* in 1917, the *Waste Land* in 1922, and particularly in the history of Eliot himself, *Ash Wednesday*, in 1930.

Prufrock's entry seemed as quiet as Charlotte Brontë's into a Victorian drawing-room, but its effect upon established traditions was even more subversive. This was the new poetry, significant, touching, poignantly here, on social problems, direct, precise in expression. The style, with its ironic juxtaposition of the colloquial and romantic, had come chiefly from France, Laforgue being his source, as Eliot tells us.

The *Waste Land* gives a survey of the futility and anarchy in contemporary history. The lowest point was reached in *The Hollow Men*. But both these poems are impersonal and dramatic; the impression remaining is not despair ; they are both distinguished by the beautiful lines, still dramatic, which light them.

After the *Waste Land*, in *For Lancelot Andrewes*, Eliot tells us he has become an Anglo-Catholic. He still sees the same chaos in life. But now he sees something of a personal solution. In *Ash Wednesday* he is struggling for an assurance of the divine. It is only in *Marina* that the soul for a moment seems to be aware of the promised land it has sought.

These last two poems are specially interesting to the historian in their exploration of the " dream-crossed twilight."

It is not only an enlargement of subject-matter, a new dignity in attitude and a new control in diction and vocabulary, which are found in his poetry, but in his criticism is strong reinforcement for these changes.

His poetry is traditional, linking the intellectual subtlety of Donne (in whom Eliot points out [1] " thought is an intense feeling, which is one with every other feeling ") with the ironically realistic style of the French symbolists.

44. *The Hollow Men* is taken from *Poems 1909–1925* (1925); 45. *Marina* from *Collected Poems 1909–1935* (1936) ; and 46. *The Soul of Man must Quicken* from *The Rock* (1934).

44. *The Hollow Men.*—The epigraph, *Mistah Kurtz—he dead*, printed, in the original text, on the half-title, is the sad and horrible climax of Conrad's great story *The Heart of Darkness*, and evokes an atmosphere which does not lift so far as the lost souls of the poem are concerned. These hollow men are like those Dante tells us of, who rushed aimlessly about in hell because they " did nothing strongly nor believed in anything but themselves." Empty and desolate therefore is their state. They fear to enter the dream kingdom, for " what dreams may come " ? They would disguise themselves as animals or scarecrows or as dead leaves

---

[1] *Homage to John Dryden.*

in the wind, for they would not be seen, nor face the judgment.   Groping and dumb they are like puppets in the final nightmare, tailing off with a whimper.

This dread and desperation are not the final impression.   It is an Inferno, but the poet-guide carries with him other airs, for the keynote is in perhaps the loveliest passage Eliot has written :

> " Eyes I dare not meet in dreams
>
> . . . .
>
> Than a fading star."

And in the last nightmare section, in spite of the sense of doom, and, worse, of futility at the miserable end, there are present, too, great powers.

The three middle sections, II–IV, touch on " the dream-crossed twilight," " the time of tension between dying and birth " in which the poems of *Ash Wednesday* move.

The eyes are referred to again in the first Minor Poem, "*Eyes that last I saw in tears.*"

45. *Marina.*

Marina, the daughter of Pericles, Prince of Tyre, was born at sea.   Her mother was said to have died and her father had her brought up at Tarsus by the governor Cleon and his wife Dionysa.   All went well until Marina came of age.   Dionysa, in jealousy, ordered Leonine to murder her.   At the coast, pirates seized her and sold her as a slave at Mytilene.   By chance Pericles landed here and saw and recognised her.   She was betrothed to the governor of Mytilene, but going to return thanks at Diana's shrine at Ephesus the priestess was discovered to be her own mother.

T. S. Eliot's *Marina* is the most recent version of the Apollonius saga, which arose in Greece and spread over nearly the whole of Europe.   Henry Morley pointed out that its parable is of universal appeal : it is " the old theme of life tossed upon the waves of Fortune, who sometimes restores all with a full hand to those who can abide the pelting of her pitiless storm. Here the wind changes at last, and . . . Pericles is left to end his life in the warm sunshine."

In English there were many treatments of the story. Shakespeare's chief source was Gower's poem, though he changed some of the names of the characters.

Quis hic locus . . . plaga ? : " What is this place, what region, what shore of the world ? "
This epigraph comes from Seneca's *Hercules*, and recalls the awful moment when the hero, having slain his children in a fit of madness, recovers his wits and sees what he has done.

unsubstantial : the new vision has rendered the old death-values unsubstantial.

I made this : i.e. in order " to construct something upon which to rejoice."

The rigging . . . caulking : but these ships I made are now to be abandoned for the new ships.

garboard strake : the outside plank next the keel.

Living to live . . . the new ships : there are suggestions here that death can be conquered, that glimpses are seen, in the mind's eye, of the promised land.

The story of Marina is a fitting symbol for this stage of the poet's pilgrimage, for the daughter of Pericles was lost but found again, and the former vision which sustained the poet in the world, the waste land, is here transcended. A new vision has been found. Its grace has made the waste land ending in death in various forms unsubstantial. A wonder grows as the new vision, this face . . . more distant than stars and nearer than the eye, leads him to abandon the ship he had made for the new ships in which to set out towards the granite islands, the new shores of the world beyond time, dimly apprehended.

RANSOM, JOHN CROWE, of Scots-Irish descent, was
born in 1888 in Pulaski, Tennessee, and educated at
Vanderbilt University, Tennessee, and, as a Rhodes
Scholar, at Oxford.   In 1914 he became a Lecturer and
later Professor in Vanderbilt University.   He served
in the American Expeditionary Force, 1917–18.   He
married and has two children.   He helped to found an
important magazine of poetry, *The Fugitive*.   His own
published works include *Poems about God*, 1919;
Chills and Fevers, 1924; *Grace after Meat*, 1924.

47, 48.   *Wrestling* and *Southern Mansion* are taken
from *Grace after Meat*, edited by Robert Graves, 1924.

Mr. Graves speaks of Ransom's " extremely fastidious
art disguised by colloquialism."   The dramatic vigour
of *Wrestling* contrasts effectively with the more delicate
ironic grace of *Southern Mansion*.   Mr. Graves explains
that this latter poem " is post-European-War Tennessee
looking at pre-Civil-War Tennessee."   His selection
omits (as indicated in the text, p. 64, by . . .) four of the
original twelve stanzas, nos, 4, 5, 7 and 9, as published
in *Chills and Fevers* (1924).

ROSENBERG, ISAAC ROSENBERG (1890–1918),   one
of eight children, was educated in Stepney and then
being apprenticed to an " art-firm," he went to evening
classes at the Art School of Birkbeck College.   Happily,
he was helped to go to the Slade School from 1911 to
1914, though he grew to think of himself first as a poet.

In 1912 he published *Night and Day*, the first of three
pamphlets of his poems, at his own expense.   In 1914
he went to seek dry air in South Africa for the benefit
of his lungs.   But he soon had to return and in 1915
enlisted.   He was killed in action in April 1918.

49. *Break of Day in the Trenches*, one of his best-known
poems, is taken from *The Collected Works of Isaac
Rosenberg* (Poetry.   Prose.   Letters and some Draw-
ings).   Edited by Gordon Bottomley and Denys
Harding.   With a Foreword by Siegfried Sassoon, 1937.

In 1922 had appeared *Poems*, by Isaac Rosenberg. Selected and edited by Gordon Bottomley with an Introductory Memoir by Laurence Binyon.

There is power and promise of more in Rosenberg's poetry.   Mr. Binyon pays tribute to his " fine intention, ardent toil and continual self-criticism."

SITWELL, OSBERT, was born in London in 1892, and educated at Eton.   He was in the Grenadier Guards from 1913 to 1919.   In *Who's Who* he explains he is " deeply interested in . . . sport," and likes to travel widely.

His publications include : in poetry [with Edith Sitwell], *Twentieth Century Harlequinade*, 1916 ;   *Argonaut and Juggernaut*, 1919 ; *Out of the Flame*, 1923 ; *Collected Satires and Poems*, 1931 ; essays, *Who Killed Cock Robin?* 1921 ; *Discursions on Travel, Art and Life*, 1925 ; *Triple Fugue and Other Stories*, 1924 ; *Dumb Animal and Other Stories*, 1930.

50. *On the Coast of Coromandel* is taken from *The Year's Poetry*, 1934 ; *The Manner* (51), from *Collected Poems*, 1931.

A quotation from *Who Killed Cock Robin?* illustrates a point of view common to the three Sitwells.   " A poem need not have a message, or a story, or a philosophy, any more than a bun need have currants.   If a bun have currants, all the better for those who like them.   But the poet must not mistake the currant for the bun." (p. 13.)

SACKVILLE-WEST, THE HON. VICTORIA, the daughter of the third Baron Sackville, was born at Knole, Sevenoaks, Kent, in 1892, and educated at home.   In 1913 she married the Hon. Harold Nicolson.

Her publications include : *Knole and the Sackvilles*, 1922 ; *Passenger to Teheran*, 1926 ; *Andrew Marvell*, 1929 ; *Saint Joan of Arc*, 1936 ; *The Edwardians* (1930, 31, 35) and *All Passion Spent* (1931), novels ; poetry, *The Land*, 1926 (Hawthornden prize, 1927) ; *Collected Poems*, 1933 ; *Pepita* [partly autobiographic], 1937.

READ, HERBERT, D.S.O. 1918, M.C., D.Litt., was born in Yorkshire in 1893 and educated at Crossley's School, Halifax, and the University of Leeds. He fought in France and Belgium, 1915–18. Afterwards he became Assistant Principal in H.M. Treasury and later Assistant Keeper in the Victoria and Albert Museum. Then he went to the University of Edinburgh as Professor of Fine Art for two years, when he became Lecturer in Art in the University of Liverpool. His publications include : *English Prose Style*, 1928 ; *The Meaning of Art*, 1931 ; *Form in Modern Poetry*, 1932 ; *Art Now*, 1933 ; *Poems*, 1914–1934 ; *In Defence of Shelley*, 1935.

Day's Affirmation (p. xx of Introduction to this book) is in *Poems* 1914–1934.

OWEN, WILFRED, was born at Plas Wilmot, Oswestry, in 1893, and educated at the Birkenhead Institute and at King's College, London. Illness in 1913 led to his going to France, and he became a tutor at Bordeaux. In 1915 he joined the Artists' Rifles, and in 1917 the Manchester Regiment, where he remained until his death on November 4, 1918.

His poems are collected in the volume from which *Futility* (54) and *Strange Meeting* (55) are taken, *The Poems of Wilfred Owen and Notices of his Life and Work*, by Edmund Blunden, 1931.

In France, Owen had studied French poetry with delight, particularly its use of assonance. This he found of the greatest use for his own verse, above all in " the solemn music of ' Strange Meeting.' " Mr. Blunden, in his *Memoir*, admirably describes its effect : " again and again by means of it he creates remoteness, darkness, emptiness, shock, echo, the last word. So complete and characteristic is his deployment of this technical resource that imitators have been few."

In his own Preface Owen wrote " My subject is War, and the pity of War. The Poetry is in the pity."

CHURCH, RICHARD, was born in London in 1893, and educated at Dulwich Hamlet School. He entered the Civil Service, but "loathed the bureaucratic machine, its capture by the highly sterilised Fabian system, and all the backstair life of government and politics," and retired in 1933. He was thus able to devote his full time to writing.

His publications include : in poetry, *Flood of Life*, 1917 ; . . . *Theme and Variations*, 1928 ; *Mood without Measure*, 1928 ; *The Glance Backward*, 1930 ; *News from the Mountain*, 1932 ; *Twelve Noon*, 1936 ; in prose, *Mary Shelley*, 1928 ; *Oliver's Daughter*, 1930 ; *High Summer*, 1931 ; *The Prodigal Father*, 1933 ; *Apple of Concord*, 1935.

He is interested in the speaking of verse, and is a director of the Oxford Festival in Spoken Poetry and also an examiner in this subject for the University of London.

56. *Mud* appeared first in *The Year's Poetry*, 1935.

57. *Secret Service* is in *The Year's Poetry*, 1937. Mr. Church tells me that the latter, " of course, is written with a *double entendre*. It can be treated as a spy story, and also as an allegory of the psychological victory of the person with an anti-social complex, the person who feels ' odd,' out of things, and misunderstood for some reason or other. The two versions coincide on the point that I believe the spy to represent a pathological condition of human society, just as the person with a secretive habit due to some inferiority feeling is also pathological."

CUMMINGS, EDWARD ESTLIN, was born in 1894 at Cambridge, Mass., and was educated at Harvard University (M.A. 1916). In 1917 he drove ambulances in France and then became a private in Camp Devens, Mass. A painter and a writer, he worked for some time in Paris, where his work in both arts became known. Returning to New York, he was awarded the *Dial* prize for literature.   His publications include *The Enormous Room*, 1922, a well-known war novel which describes his experiences in a French prison (for " an epistolary indiscretion "); poetry, *Tulips and Chimneys*, 1923; *XLI Poems*, 1925; *&*, 1925; *Is 5*, 1926; a play, *him*, in 21 scenes, 1927; By E. E. Cummings (no title), 1930: art, *CIOPW*, 1931 (Charcoal drawings, Ink drawings, Oil paintings, Pencil drawings, and Water-colours); poetry, *Viva*, 1931; *No Thanks*, 1935.   A slim volume of 28 pages is published in London, namely $\frac{1}{20}$ *Poems* by E. E. Cummings: A Selection made by the Author. *here's a little mouse* is taken from this volume.

In much of his poetry, Cummings expresses satirically the sense of waste and disillusionment after the War.

He is fond of certain verbal tricks—the splitting up of words and syllables, and an entirely individual use of capitals and punctuation—to suggest, by these sudden breaks and emphases, the exact shade of sensation required.

The method can be very effective in this light verse— in the present selection no. 58, *Four III*, as in the well-known poems on the motor-crash or the jazz tempo of electric signs.

PORTER, ALAN, born in Indianapolis, in 1899, was educated at Manchester Grammar School and Queen's College, Oxford.   He is a lecturer in English in Vassar College, Poughkeepsie, New York State.   He published *The Signature of Pain and Other Poems* in 1930.
59. *The River* is a charming " Insect Play " in little.

BLUNDEN, EDMUND CHARLES (born 1896), educated at Christ's Hospital and Queen's College, Oxford. He served in the War in France and Belgium as lieutenant with the Royal Sussex Regt. (M.C.). He was Professor of English Literature, Tokyo University, 1924–27.   He was awarded the Hawthornden Prize in 1922, and the Royal Society of Literature medal 1930. He was Fellow and Tutor, Merton College, Oxford, from 1931. His publications include : *The Waggoner and Other Poems*, 1920 ; *Poems, 1914–30* ; *Half-Way House*, 1932 ; *Choice or Chance*, 1934 ; *An Elegy and other Poems*, 1936 ; in prose, *The Bonadventure*, 1922 ; *On the Poems of Henry Vaughan*, 1927 ; *Leigh Hunt's Examiner*, 1928 ; *Undertones of War*, 1928, in the Penguin Library 1937 ; *Nature in English Literature*, 1929 ; *Life of Leigh Hunt*, 1930 ; *The Face of England*, 1932 ; *Charles Lamb and his Contemporaries*, 1934 ; *The Mind's Eye*, 1934 ; (with Sylva Norman) *We'll Shift our Ground*, 1933, and many other publications.

60. *Lark Descending* comes from *Choice or Chance*.

GRAVES, ROBERT, was born in London in 1895 of mixed parentage, Irish-Scottish-Danish-German. He had a Classical education interrupted by the War, in which he served with the Royal Welch Fusiliers in France ; being wounded and left for dead during the capture of High Wood on the Somme, officially reported died of wounds on his twenty-first birthday. He married young, resumed his education, which so far consisted only of Latin, Greek and a little mathematics, by slowly training himself to write clear English. After the War he took a degree at Oxford, and except for a year as Professor of English Literature at Cairo University in 1926 has always since avoided taking any job that would compromise his independence. He lives by writing. He has four children. He is more widely known by the books which he writes to make money than by his poems, which he regards as his real work. He has collaborated with Laura Riding in several critical books and two novels, and worked with her as a printer.

His published works include : *Poems, 1914–26* ; *Poems, 1926–30* ; *Poems, 1930–33* ; with Laura Riding,

A Survey of Modernist Poetry, 1927, and *A Pamphlet against Anthologies*, 1928 ; *Goodbye to All That, An Autobiography*, 1929 ; *But it still Goes On, A Miscellany*, 1930 ; *The Real David Copperfield*, 1933 ; *I, Claudius*, 1934 (awarded the Hawthornden and James Tait Black Prizes for 1934) ; *Claudius the God*, 1934 ; *Antigua Penny Puce*, 1936 ; *Count Belisarius*, 1938. He is Associate Editor of *Epilogue*. His *Collected Poems* are to appear in the autumn, 1938. *Broken Images* appeared in *Poems 1926–30* ; *Time* and *The Legs* in *Poems 1930–1933* ; *To Walk on Hills* appeared in *Epilogue*, Spring 1937.

One stanza from an early poem which Robert Graves has suppressed, I should like to rescue from oblivion :

> But may the gift of heavenly peace
> And glory for all time
> Keep the boy Tom who tending geese
> First made the nursery rhyme.

64. *The Wretch*, hitherto unpublished, tells of someone who relied on the official court-poet tradition of poetry (the Sun-god was the official patron of all laureates) to support him, instead of remaining a poet in his own right. The official tradition has collapsed at last, and is here seen in all its petulant shabbiness.

66. *The Exile* appeared in *Epilogue*, Summer 1936. This dramatic poem is an effective picture of exile. When someone withdraws himself from intimate relations with the society into which he was born, and cultivates his mind apart, people take revenge by imposing an official exile on him. His actions acquire an unnecessary mysteriousness, especially as he does not regard the exile as seriously as he is expected to do.

The Regency period makes a convenient setting for this conception of exile. The peer is a mysterious personage who might have been connected with the Prince Regent's circle. He occupies himself By night at his old work, probably with writing epigrams and black or white magic.   Many of his kind are described in Gronow's *Memoirs* 1889, or in *The Regency Rakes* by E. Beresford Chancellor, 1925.

RIDING, LAURA, was born January 16, 1901, in New York City.   She has published books of criticism and story, besides books of poems ; regards poems as the most important form of life.   Since she appears in the anthology as the author of poems, she considers that biographical details would be inappropriate, as belonging to mere physical living.   She believes in close co-operation in thought between poets, and practises this.   In her view, however, the number of co-operative-minded poets is comparatively small.   Many poets today fail to be real poets, because they do not work or think hard enough.

The clues to all the fundamental problems of life are to be found in poetry, she insists : and now that life brings people face to face with these, poets have greater responsibilities than ever before.

She is editor of *Epilogue*, a critical series, and director of *The Seizen Press*.

Among her publications are : *Poems : A Joking Word*, 1930 ; *Poems : A Lying Word*, 1931 ; *The Life of the Dead* (poems in French and English, with woodcuts), 1933 ; *A Survey of Modernist Poetry*, 1927, and *A Pamphlet against Anthologies*, 1928 (these two with Robert Graves) ; *Anarchism is not Enough* (essays), 1928 ; *Everybody's Letters*, 1933 ; *Progress of Stories*, 1935 ; *A Trojan Ending* (novel), 1937. *Collected Poems* appeared in the Spring, 1938. 67. *The Quids* appeared in *Poems : A Joking Word* ; 68. *As Many Questions as Answers* and 69. *Earth* in *Poems : A Lying Word*. Nos. 70–72, *Doom in Bloom*, *The Victory*, and *After So Much Loss* are here published for the first time.

67. *The Quids*. This brilliant poem, a kind of philosophical satire, can be enjoyed entirely, and rightly, for

its lively self. It should be welcome particularly to those interested in the worlds of grammar, logic or metaphysics. Laura Riding has kindly written the following note for me on the *Monoton*, the aggregative name of the quids' " home." She says : " The poem might be described as a story about how there began to be *activity* in existence. It begins on a philosophical vein, ironically—but almost immediately, as the sense of activity is developed in the poem, the irony fades and there is complete concentration on rendering the effect of existence busily alive everywhere in itself. This ' itself ' is the Monoton (in the Greek it would be Monōton—but in the form Mónoton it has the suggestion of Monotony). The somewhat ironic character is due to the fact that of course one cannot give a complete picture of existence in terms of activity : hence the grotesqueness of identifying the general character of existence, as opposed to the particular, with inactivity —i.e. mono-sameness."

gisty : of gist, the pith of the matter.

thoughtfall : as happy a coinage as " monoton " itself.

70. *Doom in Bloom.*

Hurries to take the separate colour: we seek individuality.

from the deep bed of ultimate misgiving : from the depths of hesitant ancient being where life was not sure of what it would turn into.

similar smiles : a happy fellow-feeling of all sharing exactly the same losses and failures.

71. *The Victory.*

battalions of fire : fire seen as advancing like an army, in massed conflagrations.

the embattled minds : the insensitive minds seen as in fighting formation against knowledge.

the voices of time : all the " modern " talk now going on.

a love . . . in a heart . . . gloved : namely, a love that holds its tenderness in, so that it is not wasted on what it could not move.

When poets have an exact consciousness of what is happening in the making of a poem, their comments on poetry are the closest we can get in the way of a prose statement of the meaning of poetry. Careful readers of poems may also say interesting things about what poetry means to them, and such statements can be valuable in helping us to develop sensitivity in our own reading. We ought to be especially grateful for statements of the first kind ; and I am therefore glad to be able to give the following precise account by Laura Riding of the kind of thought the writing of a poem involves.

Her view of what a poem is—and a view to which poets associated with her subscribe (Robert Graves, James Reeves, Norman Cameron and some others)—differs markedly from the view held by many of her contemporaries ; as, in consequence, the way in which she writes poems differs from theirs. With this view also goes a special sense of what it is to be a poet. The difference between her attitude to poetry and that of the majority of contemporary poets is, in fact, that she regards a poet as dedicated very literally to the work of reconciling the separate things, the separate kinds of reality, into which existence is broken up—of finding the way in which they can truly be reconciled.

To her a poet is not merely a writer who feels things more vividly than other people and describes them in a way to excite other people about them : a poet to her is responsible for making existence be as good as it can be, for relating one part of it to another in the most harmonious way that can also be a permanent way.

A poem, in her view, is therefore not merely a piece of very exciting or pleasurable writing, but a solemn act of unification which is also a completely pleasant act because it brings things together by some quality that they have in common, however different they may be.   She would say that it is the poet's task to clarify the general qualities that particular things must have in common, if they belong within the frame of existence.

So in her poems we find general statements and particular descriptions in startlingly close combinations. For example, if there were a reference to a particular kind of weather, there would probably also be something to indicate generally what weather is, in relation to some other general experience that people have—it might be the experience of remembering the past. And then perhaps, some special happening in the past would be described, and, in turn, the meaning of this would be indicated in relation to all past experience : and then the meaning of all past experience in relation to every immediate event.

And we might be made to feel the place that memory of the past had in all present experience : and how a particular kind of weather did or did not combine with a particular memory, or a particular present experience.

Finally, perhaps, we might see how, when our thoughts were restless, driven by contemplation of the restless weather to comparisons between the past and the present, they turned to the future in escape from the restlessness of the present.

And we should then be ready to understand something very important and interesting about ourselves : for example, that our thoughts of the future really belonged to the present, even in being safe from memory changes, which pull back to the past, and from weather changes, which pull towards the future.

At any rate it would all tie up somehow in some very precise way that would also be a permanent way of thinking about the things brought together in the poem. And the atmosphere of the poem would be intimate, because things were brought into such fundamentally close contact : but not because of any personal revelations.

A poem, in Laura Riding's view, must not be just a revelation about the poet's emotions or personal experiences : the poet is a revealer of everything, not just a self-revealer.

This quality of intimacy which her poems have without being intimate personal confessions, is not so strikingly apparent in any other poet, I believe, except Chaucer ; and the poets associated with her also have this Chaucerian freshness of language, which is not to be confused with the informal autobiographical language that so many modern poets use.

ROBERTS, MICHAEL (1902), was educated at Bournemouth School and King's College, London, and Trinity College, Cambridge. In 1935 he married Janet Adam Smith and has one son. His publications include *Poems*, Cape, 1936 ; *Critique of Poetry*, 1934 ; *The Modern Mind*, 1937. *New Signatures*, 1932, an anthology of new poems ; *The Faber Book of Modern Verse*, 1937. *T. E. Hulme* was published in the Spring, 1938.

73. *Wir Sind Alle Verloren* (We are all lost men) is the third of the five sections of *Elegy for the Fallen Climbers*. From *Poems*, 1936.

Nanga Parbat : Simla, July 23, 1934. Three members of the German Himalayan expedition, Herr Merkel the leader, Dr. Wieland and Dr. Welzenbach and seven coolies perished in a blizzard while climbing Nanga Parbat (26,628 feet) in the Kashmir Himalaya.

Angtsering : a very brave porter who was nearly killed in this expedition. His picture is in Fritz Bechtold's *Nanga Parbat Adventure*, 1935.

Bennen : J. J. Bennen (1824–64) was one of the most famous of all the early guides. He accompanied Tyndall regularly, and was with him when they made the first ascent of the Weisshorn. He was killed during a winter climb on the Haut-de-Cry, 1864. This is a mountain between Lausanne and Brig, in Valais, a canton of Switzerland.

Carrel : Jean-Antoine Carrel was the chief guide of

Edward Whymper, the famous mountaineer. His death, later, from exhaustion, on the Matterhorn " after bringing his employers into safety through a snowstorm forms one of the noblest pages in the history of mountaineering " (*Ency. Brit.*). Sinigglia, the engineer, and the two guides Carrel and Gorret, without food or drink had been sheltering under a rock for 36 hours. But the cold became unbearable. They resolved on a final struggle with death. But Carrel began to weaken and died in spite of all they could do. The cord binding them had become solid ice. Gorret's pocket was frozen, and he could not cut him loose until they met a rock rising from the ice and his axe then did it. Gorret still speaks of the experience as of the other world and cannot explain how he escaped Carrel's fate.

tourmente : a French word used by Alpinists, meaning a storm, violent but brief.

74. *In Time of Peace.*

Langres : The Plateau de Langres is in the French departments Haute-Marne and Côte d'Or and Haut-Saône, and has 1,695 feet altitude.

Macugnaga : this is in Piedmont in Italy, under Monte Rosa.

Bruno : Giordano Bruno (c. 1548–1600) was a Dominican interested in Renaissance philosophy and a follower of Copernicus. His views were frowned on as impious and he fled from Rome in 1576. After lecturing in Paris he had two years in England, 1583–5, happy in being free to write under Elizabeth. After returning to the Continent he rashly went to Venice, where the officers of the Inquisition imprisoned him. In 1593 he was taken to Rome and kept in prison till his death at the stake in 1600.

Jules, Marcel and Guillaume : any three soldiers in the Chasseurs Alpins, on the Franco-Italian frontier near the Col de la Galise, a well-known chamois country, where poaching still goes on.

The Paramount : any big cinema outwardly imposing, but its foundations are as frail as those of all human structures.

75. *The Castle.*—I asked Mr. Roberts about the tree of blackness and he kindly gave the following account :

" When I wrote ' the tree of blackness falls ' I was, I believe, thinking mainly of the effect of an explosion, like the explosion of the mines beneath the Alcazar— the great column of smoke, with the cloud on top, that stands for a moment like a tree and then falls, and the debris falls with it. There is the idea of annihilation growing, too, but then itself failing.

" The castle is, I think, both an actual material castle that is defended, and a set of beliefs that makes men defend it. It is destroyed, but the ghost of it stays, partly because the heroism of the men stays in our minds and is admired even if we neither know nor care what they died for, and partly because ideas and instincts, whether right or wrong, cannot be killed just by killing the people in whom they are most prominent. Even when we think it is all finished the old instincts are there, overlaid perhaps, but not destroyed, and they are capable of forming the basis for a new enthusiasm, whether we like it or not."

Mr. Roberts continued discussing interpretations of poetry, and said : " A good poem generally turns out to be rich in meanings, and it is safe to say that the poet never saw any of them clearly as his ' intended ' meaning when he wrote. Like the reader, he felt that there was a lot in this particular form of words. Of course, this kind of richness does not by itself prove that the poem is good."

One of the possible " meanings " seems to me that the castle symbolises the old systems, old faiths and standards. These were evolved by humanity after many efforts, so that men became, as it were, old in the effort. Mankind, that is, was old (not like the young, immortal Greeks of Symonds's fancy) when the

" system " (one or another) was " finished." Then it was taken for granted, and now it is empty and broken down.

In the third stanza the War may be suggested. And then we see how things go on again. In spite of this we are haunted by the death and the unfulfilled perfection of systems bound to us intimately by long tradition.

The issue is come to be one of peace or death. Let us start again.

TESSIMOND, A. S. J., was born in Birkenhead, Cheshire, in 1902, and educated at Liverpool University. He has published one book of verse, *The Walls of Glass*, and contributes poems to periodicals, and to anthologies such as *Poems of To-morrow* and *The Year's Poetry*, 1937.

76. *La Marche des Machines* appeared in *New Signatures*, 1932. This was suggested by a Russian film. Both in subject and in its precise representation of mechanical motion the poem is a concentrated example of the contemporary interest in the internal-combustion engine, evident in many fields of thought and action.

LEWIS, CECIL DAY, was born in Ireland in 1904, and educated at Sherborne School and Wadham College, Oxford. He edited *Oxford Poetry* (with W. H. Auden) in 1927, and then began to teach at Oxford, Helensburgh and at Cheltenham College. His publications include : *A Hope for Poetry*, 1934, and 1936 ; *Collected Poems, 1929–1933*, 1935 ; *A Time to Dance*, 1935 ; *Noah and the Waters*, 1936 ; and several novels, of which the last is *Starting Point*, 1936.

77. *Live you by love confined* is no. 14 in the group of poems called *The Magnetic Mountain*, first published in 1933.

78. *A Time to Dance* is the introductory poem to the book of the same name.

CAMERON, NORMAN, was born in Bombay, India, in 1905, and educated at Fettes College and at Oriel College, Oxford. He has published a book of poems, *The Winter House*, in 1935, and is preparing a book of translations of the poems of Arthur Rimbaud.

He contributes poems to *Epilogue* and to *New Verse.*
79. *Moonlight, Waterlight and Opal* has been taken from *Epilogue*, Spring 1937.

Corinthians : the term has here its early nineteenth century sense of elegant dissipation, slightly sinister dandyism. A practical example will make one meaning plain. One night I was staring at some enchanting sprays of Traveller's Joy in a clear rainbow-tinted vase, the whole reflected in a Queen Anne mirror, and suddenly turned from it in disgust, thoroughly corrupting I felt the sight ; a fatal will-o'-the-wisp luring me from copying out the tangled draft due for the post. Everyone ought to learn *Moonlight, Waterlight and Opal* by heart !

BOTTRALL, (FRANCIS JAMES) RONALD, was born at Camborne, Cornwall, in 1906, and educated at Redruth County School and Pembroke College, Cambridge. He won the Charles Oldham Shakespeare Scholarship in 1927. He first became Lector in English at the University of Helsingfors, Finland, until 1931, when he went to Princeton University, U.S.A., with a Commonwealth Fund Fellowship. In 1933 he became Johore Professor of English Language and Literature at Raffles College, Singapore, and in 1938 Assistant Director of The British Institute, Florence.

He has published *The Loosening and Other Poems*, 1931; *Festivals of Fire* (poems), 1935; *Crooked Eclipses* (poems).

The Thyrsus Retipped (see p. xix of Introduction to this book) and nos. 80 and 81 are in *The Loosening*.

The thyrsus was an emblem of Dionysus, a staff or spear, with an ornament like a pine-cone at the top, and sometimes wrapped with ivy or vine branches.

Dionysus, in Greek mythology, originally a nature god of fruitfulness and vegetation, especially of the vine, and hence the god of wine, possessed also the gift of prophecy. The drama, both in tragedy and comedy, originated in performances in his honour at the Dionysia, his games in Attica (see the *Ency. Brit.*).

" What relevance today " asks the poet, " have the themes that excited earlier poets ? "   At first he turns to minute introspection, but in vain.   For a time he is quiescent.   Certainly in these days there may be any detailed examination of frail and ephemeral things from zoology to beauty ; or there is machinery ; but all these are as yet emotionally chill.   There are hints for new beginnings in the normal experiences of life.   These are not the end.

Prosthesis is contrasted with epitaphs in the last line.   With the whole stanza compare Dryden's

> The pointed hour of promis'd Bliss
> The pleasing whisper in the dark,
> The half unwilling willing kiss,
> The laugh that guides thee to the mark.
> When the kind Nymph wou'd coyness feign,
> And hides but to be found again ;
> These, these are joys the Gods for Youth ordain.

[Transl. of 9th ode of first book of Horace, l. 32, st. vi. Oxford ed., pp. 403–4.]

Anangke : Gr. ἀνάγκη, necessity.

Valéry : a leading French poet and critic.   Paul Valéry began as a follower of Mallarmè, whose daughter he married in 1917.   Very clear accounts of Valéry and of Joyce are given in *Axel's Castle*, by Edmund Wilson, 1931.

ephemerides : ephemera = insect living only a day. (Cf. O.E.D. under *ephemeris*, 5.)

microscopic anatomy of ephemerides : the whole line can be taken to mean any detailed examination of zoology, or of frail and ephemeral things —such as (even) beauty.

> prosthesis : (in its surgical sense) "that part which fills up what is wanting " (O.E.D.), hence, beginning again.

80. *The Future is Not for Us.*

From out the middle west : of America.

81. *Arion Anadyomenos.*

Arion was a lyric poet and musician in the island of Lesbos.   He went into Italy with Periander, the tyrant of Corinth.   Later, he wished to revisit his native city. But the sailors, envious of the riches he was carrying to Lesbos, arranged to murder him.   Arion begged he might first play a tune.   When it was finished, he plunged into the sea. Some dolphins had been attracted by his music, and one of them bore him safely to Tænarus whence he hastened to Periander's court.

Arion Anadyomenos is a complement to *The Future is Not for Us* : here the recognition of stress and crisis is cheered only by determination.   But its uncertain hope becomes strengthened and joyous in the splendid rhythms which close *Arion Anadyomenos.*

It is interesting to notice how effectively Shakespearean phrases are used in these poems, the **spies of fortune, childed on our fears, down the wind,** and many more.

> **Anadyomenos:** Anadyomene applied to Venus, meaning emerging from the sea.   Apelles, the painter, made a famous picture of this.

> **the toothless beldam :** an old woman of character. Although toothless she was always ready to exert her jaws on anything eatable and her brain on any argument, however tough.

> **remainder biscuit :** Touchstone's brain was " dry as the remainder biscuit after a voyage . . ." (*A.Y.L.I.* II. vii 37).

> **Zaccheus :** a chief publican of Jericho who entertained Christ.   He climbed into a tree the better to see Him (Luke xix. 1-10).

A dove content with his olive branch : the house is thought of as an ark.   The dove suggests the Holy Ghost.

sworn foe to the syllogist : that is, to anyone who chops logic.

that uneasiness in us and Reactions to . . . a vocal cord : the strong consciousness in poets and musicians.

cerement : wrappings.

passacaglia : an early Italian or Spanish dance.   The music is constructed on a ground bass of 2, 4, or 8 bars.   It has a solemn character.   (Cf. Grove's *Dictionary of Music and Musicians*, 1928.)

Some stony replica : not a reproduction in terms of a stiff, outworn art-form, but in terms of something living and vital—all this making for a freer life.

What song the sirens sang : a symbol for an " insuperable " obstacle overcome, for an " impenctrablc " jungle opened.

" What song the Syrens sang, or what name Achilles assumed when he hid himself among women, though puzzling questions, are not beyond all conjecture."— Sir Thomas Browne, *Hydriotaphia* (Urn-Burial), chap. v.

82. *Preamble to a Great Adventure* is here first published in its present form.   This fine poem is a satire on the mass-produced type of " Empire Builder."

panatrope : amplifier, loud-speaker.

colour : the race problem.

cleft palate : affectations of speech.

grooves as spirals : such mass-produced puppets are assured that the grooves in which they have been moulded are very good for them, because they are really spirals.

timid leprosies . . . endless probings . . . : uncomfortable or bad dreams, and uncontrolled mental wanderings.

squid : cuttle-fish.

amputation : death.

AUDEN, WYSTAN HUGH, born 1907, was educated at Gresham's School, Holt, and Christ Church, Oxford. The significant part in his education is described by Christopher Isherwood in *New Verse*, November 1937 : " Science, music and ritualism and the sagas (his family came from Iceland originally) most influenced him." Much other biographical information, and literary comments by his contemporaries in poetry, as well as a check-list of his writings, are given in this " Auden Double Number." The list includes *Poems*, 1930 ; *The Orators*, 1932 ; *Poems*, 1932 ; *The Dance of Death* (with C. Isherwood), 1933 ; *The Dog Beneath the Skin* (with C. Isherwood), 1935 ; *The Poet's Tongue*, An Anthology with John Garrett, 1935 ; *The Ascent of F6* (with C. Isherwood), 1936 ; *Look, Stranger !* 1936 ; *Spain* (a short poem), 1937 ; *Letters from Iceland* (with Louis MacNeice), 1937. The King's Medal was awarded to Auden in 1937.

83. *The Witnesses* was first printed in *The Listener* : here, it is taken from *Poems of To-Morrow*, 1935.

The " Witnesses " are the two witnesses of the Apocalypse.

> And I will give power unto my two witnesses, and they shall prophesy. . . . And if any man will hurt them, fire proceedeth out of their mouth, and devoureth their enemies. . . . And their dead bodies shall lie in the street of the great city, which spiritually is called Sodom and Egypt, where also our Lord was crucified. . . . And they that dwell upon the earth shall rejoice over them . . . because these two prophets tormented them that dwelt on the earth.

(Rev. xi. 3, 5, 8, 10.)

Prince Alpha, with every opportunity and every acquirement, was entirely unconscious of one matter, responsibility to others, and he died of boredom.

85. *Letter to Lord Byron*, Part V.

Yeats has helped himself to Parnell's heart : see *Parnell's Funeral*, by W. B. Yeats, *The Year's Poetry* in 1936.

> ... nor did we play a part
> Upon a painted stage when we devoured his heart.

Wyndham Lewis: see his recent autobiography, *Blasting and Bombadiering*, 1937.

Es neiget die Weisen zu Schönen sich: Wise men pay tribute to beauty.

The Withered State: so called in the *Communist Manifesto*.

Wolf's Goethe-lieder: this is Hugo Wolf's *Gedichte von Goethe für eine Singstimme und Clavier*, composed 1888–1889.

Ganymede: this refers to Schubert's Op. 19, no. 3.

Lord Alfred . . . Arthur: these are Lord Alfred Douglas and Sir Arthur Pinero.

clerihew: Mr. E. C. Bentley kindly gave me the following first definition of this term : " You ask me about Clerihews In 1905 I published a book of nonsense rhymes called *Biography for Beginners* illustrated by G K Chesterton . . . It was published under the name of E. Clerihew my own baptismal names being Edmund Clerihew . . .

" In course of time this form of nonsense became popular among connoisseurs Somebody began to call such rhymes Clerihews I never knew who began this The rhymes were imitated by many people. Some made excellent imitations . . .

" I never thought of such a thing as a definition of a Clerihew It is a four line verse about some historical personage the first two lines forming a rhymed couplet and the second two doing the same, there is no metric arrangement but there should always be a certain rhythm a point which is missed by most of the imitators

" *A correct Clerihew is*

> The people of Spain think Cervantes
> Equal to half a dozen Dantes
> An opinion resented most bitterly
> By the people of Italy

" *Another*
    Sir Humphry Davy
    Detested gravy
    He lived in the odium
    Of having discovered sodium

" Now I have told you all about this art form "

EMPSON, WILLIAM, was born in 1907, and educated at Winchester and Magdalene College, Cambridge, where he took first his Mathematical Tripos, and then his English one. He is now Professor of English Literature at the University of Pekin. His publications include *The Seven Types of Ambiguity* (in poetry), 1930, and *Poems*, 1935.

86. *Legal Fiction* is taken from *Poems*, 1935. It is a fascinating parallel between rights in law and the rights of the mind.

MACNEICE, LOUIS, was born in 1907, and educated at Marlborough and at Merton College, Oxford. He became Lecturer in Classics at the University of Birmingham, until 1936, when he was appointed Lecturer in Greek at Bedford College. His publications include *Blind Fireworks* (poems), 1929 ; the section on modern poetry in *The Arts of To-day*, 1935 ; on Sir Thomas Malory in *The English Novelists*, 1935 ; *Poems*, 1935 ; *The Agamemnon of Aeschylus*, translated by L. Mac-Neice, 1936, and, with Auden, *Letters from Iceland*, 1936 ; an article on *Subject in Modern Poetry* in *Essays and Studies*, 1936 ; *The Outer Hebrides*, 1937.

87. *Song* appeared first in *The Listener*, and was reprinted in *The Year's Poetry*, 1937.

88. *The Creditor* is taken from *Poems*, 1935. In *Carrion Comfort* more terribly, here more tranquilly, yet also penetratively, we are aware of the Hound of Heaven.

89. *Eclogue by a Five-Barred Gate* also comes from *Poems*, 1935. It is an effective piece of dramatic reading. Not as a whole, of course, but in one detail, it

is very slightly a skit on escapist pastoral poetry, in the shepherds' talk, now cultivated, now peasant-like. In English, the pastoral has been always artificial, " the townsman's dream of country-life." Cf. E. K. Chambers, *English Pastorals*, 1906, or W. W. Greg, *Pastoral Poetry and Pastoral Drama*, 1906.

LEHMANN, JOHN, was born at Bourne End, in the Thames Valley, in 1907, and was educated at Eton (King's Scholar) and Trinity College, Cambridge. He has published two books of poetry, *A Garden Revisited*, 1931, and *The Noise of History*, 1934, and a book about the Caucasus, *Prometheus and the Bolsheviks*, 1937. He is the Editor of *New Writing*, which appears every six months, and was co-editor of *The Year's Poetry* in 1934, '35 and '36. He also writes on Central European subjects for a number of English and American periodicals.

90. *This Excellent Machine* is taken from *New Signatures*, 1932.

91. *A Little Distance Off* comes from *Poems of To-Morrow*, 1935.

RAINE, KATHLEEN J. (Mrs. Charles Madge), was born in 1908, and educated at Girton College where she took her Natural Sciences Tripos (in biology).

92. *Fata Morgana* first appeared in *New Verse* (to which she has contributed poems) and is now reprinted as part III of the poem of that name in *The Year's Poetry*, 1937. The title *Fata Morgana*, " a kind of mirage," fitly suggests the dream which the poem is.

SPENDER, STEPHEN, was born in London in 1909, and educated at University College School, London, and University College, Oxford. He married in 1936. He first published *20 Poems*, 1930; then *Poems*, 1933; *The Destructive Element*, 1935; *The Burning Cactus*, 1936.

93. *I think continually*, and 94. *In 1929*, are both taken from *Poems*, 1933.

94. One of the subjects of the poem is the separation or
the union of lives.
  lipping skulls on the revolving rim : implies lives
    together (lipping, kissing; revolving rim, rotating
    earth).
  posture of genius : implies separate life.

REEVES, JAMES, was born at Harrow-on-the-Hill in
  1909, and educated at Stowe School and Jesus College,
  Cambridge. He has been teaching English in Canter-
  bury, London and Chichester successively. He has
  published poems in *Epilogue* and one book of poems,
  The Natural Need, 1936.
94. *Climbing a Mountain* is in *The Natural Need*.
95. *Visitors to the Waterfall* is now first published.

KEMP, HARRY V., was born in Singapore in 1911, and
  educated at Stowe, Buckingham, and at Clare College,
  Cambridge. He taught natural sciences 1931–34. He
  is at present engaged on a book about Left-wing
  politics, being himself an ex-Left.
97. *Shakespeare and Later* is now first published.

MADGE, CHARLES, was born in Johannesburg in 1912
  and educated at Winchester and Magdalene College,
  Cambridge. He originated, and is a leader in, the Mass
  Observation movement (1937). He has had poems in
  New Verse and *The Criterion*, and in anthologies. In
  1937 he published *Disappearing Castle*, a volume of
  poetry. *Blocking the Pass* (98) is in *Poems of To-Morrow*.
    This poem will be you if you will. . . . (See p. xvii
  of Introduction to this book), was published first in *The
  Listener*. Charles Madge's sonnet first reinforces Hop-
  kins's advice to read a poem aloud by a recommenda-
  tion to take it at high speed, and, secondly, recalls
  Coleridge's golden maxim . . . " that willing sus-
  pension of disbelief for the moment which constitutes
  poetic faith " (*Biographia Literaria*, 14). For Madge

counsels us, Give yourself up to the poem (let you be all . . .), not just as an onlooker (a fraction) ; if you make one violent effort like throwing a stone into a lake, and if that is all there is, then your effort is wasted and dead.

98. *Blocking the Pass.* This definite and well-controlled poem of a dramatic scene is a dream-poem. Some of Madge's poems originated thus, in dreams, but it is not true of the others. He is writing a book on the subject.

Particularly since the War much interest has been shown in those parts of the mind " below " or " beyond " the level of consciousness. The Symbolists since Baudelaire in 1847 and the Surrealists since about 1922, in more extreme manifestations have expressed their belief that the unconscious, and dreams, have " news " of value for us.

Axel's Castle, by Edmund Wilson, 1930 and 1935, gives a clear account of Symbolism, and a brief one of Surrealism. For the latter see *Surrealism,* edited by Herbert Read, 1935.

99. *The Loves of the Lions.* In the moonlit landscape there are thought-provoking contrasts : the primeval animal strife at night, and the cessation of human activity whether in an aeroplane landing or in humans asleep : the irrelevancy of the aeroplanes and iron stacks to the ancient life of the desert : and, curiously, the moonlight which brings alive the smooth-eyed statue of a woman (one of the broken statues lying about) but turns the sleeping woman into a smooth-faced statue. On the poem's dream-character, Mr. Madge sent this comment : " Though dreamlike, the poem is also African history ; it is about both past and future, and part of it has ' come true ' since it was written."

THOMAS, DYLAN, was born in Swansea in 1914, and was educated at Swansea Grammar School. He contributes poems, stories and reviews to English, Welsh and

American periodicals. He has published *18 Poems*, 1934 and *25 Poems*, 1936.

100. *The hand that signed the paper felled a city* is taken from *25 Poems*.

DYMENT, CLIFFORD, was born in 1914, and educated at Loughborough Grammar School. He has published *First Day*, 1935, and *Straight or Curly*, 1937.

101. *A Switch cut in April* comes from *Straight or Curly*.

HODGE, ALAN, was born at Scarborough in 1915, and was educated at Liverpool and at Oriel College, Oxford. A friend comments that for him being a poet is a sufficiently adventurous occupation, and therefore he has not been tempted to the usual young-poet excitements.

102. *Waiting* is taken from *Epilogue*, Spring 1937.

GASCOYNE, DAVID, was born in 1916, and educated at Salisbury Cathedral Choir School, and the Regent Street Polytechnic. His occupation is writing. He has published *Opening Day* (novel), 1933 ; *A Short History of Surrealism*, 1935 ; *Man's Life is this Meat* (poems), 1936. He contributes poems to *New Verse, Contemporary Poetry and Prose, The Listener*, and other papers. He also has poems in various anthologies, including *Recent Poetry 1923–33, Poems of To-morrow, The Faber Book of Modern Verse*, and *The Year's Poetry* for 1934, –35, –36, –37. He is at present working on a biography of Arthur Rimbaud.

103. *The Unattained* is taken from *Poems of To-Morrow*, 1935.

104. *Orpheus in the Underworld* is here first published. Mr. Gascoyne tells me : " It is from a new series of religious— or ' metaphysical '—poems on the theme of Death. *Orpheus in the Underworld* is not meant to be a transcription of the Orpheus legend, but an allegory of the spiritual condition of the twentieth-century poet. . . . It was originally written as part of a sequence

called 'Hölderlin's Madness,' and refers to the poet
Hölderlin exiled to the underworld of insanity." At
the same time it has the above general reference " to
the poet in the world of to-day."

Johann C. F. Hölderlin (1770–1843) was a German
poet, and a neo-Hellenist, translating Greek plays, and
working to bring the Greek spirit into German litera-
ture. In 1806 he " became harmlessly insane," and
remained so until his death.

INDEX OF FIRST LINES